Fundamental
Motor Patterns

Fundamental Motor Patterns

RALPH L. WICKSTROM
Ripon College, Ripon, Wisconsin

SECOND EDITION

Lea & Febiger • *Philadelphia* • *1977*

Health, Human Movement, and Leisure Studies

Ruth Abernathy, Ph.D.
Editorial Adviser
Professor Emeritus, School of Physical and Health Education
University of Washington, Seattle 98105

Library of Congress Cataloging in Publication Data

Wickstrom, Ralph L
  Fundamental motor patterns.

  Includes bibliographies and index.
  1. Physical education for children. 2. Motor
ability. 3. Child development. I. Title.
GV443.W47 1977   372.8'6   76-53536
ISBN 0-8121-0583-4

Published in Great Britain by Henry Kimpton Publishers, London

PRINTED IN THE UNITED STATES OF AMERICA

Print Number: 3 2 1

PREFACE

This book has been revised extensively to incorporate new material on fundamental motor patterns and to deal more explicitly with approaches to motor pattern development. There is not a large amount of new material on fundamental skills, but much of what is new is of relatively high quality and includes additional longitudinal data. The interpretation of developmental changes currently is more clearly defined in terms of stages and trends, and reference is made to both of these interpretations in nearly every chapter.

On the recommendation of Frank Smoll and others who have used the first edition of this book, a new chapter on walking has been added. The inclusion of walking was intended to add continuity to the study of locomotion by starting at an earlier level. The chapter on walking rightfully takes its place near the beginning of the book and serves to illustrate the specific ways in which several basic principles of motor development operate.

Attempts to put information concerning motor pattern development into a form that can be used directly by classroom and specialist teachers are discussed, and examples of some proposed plans have been included. The popular emphasis on transforming knowledge into a practical form will be seen throughout this edition, especially in connection with skill analysis. At the end of each chapter, there are additional suggestions for analyzing motor patterns by direct visual observation.

The study of motor pattern development is still relatively new, and much remains to be learned. In the next few years, there probably will be an enormous increase in knowledge because the means for studying motor development are more readily available and the interest in using them seems to be more widespread.

It is hoped that this revised edition will contribute to the expansion of knowledge by being provocative as well as practical. Perhaps it will foster respect for a critical approach to the blending of theory and practice in this important area of study.

Ripon, Wisconsin   R. L. WICKSTROM

CONTENTS

Fundamental
Motor Patterns

1

INTRODUCTION

Where there is life, there is movement; where there are children, there is almost perpetual movement. Children normally run, jump, throw, catch, kick, strike, and perform a multitude of basic skills. They learn these first as general skills and later in modified versions as specific sport skills. They combine the skills into patterns of increasingly greater specificity and complexity. This continuing process of motor skill development seems to take place in a varying degree regardless of whether adults do anything to help or to hinder it. The improvement can be explained partly in terms of increased capability that accompanies growth and development and partly in terms of a natural, untutored process that results from imitation, trial and error, and freedom of movement. This natural process often produces Topsy-like skill development that represents lost opportunities for progress of a much higher order. Specifically, it falls far short of what might be considered optimum motor skill development.

The concept of optimum skill development has been in existence for many years, but its lofty possibilities have escaped serious notice. The idea of optimum development is grandiose and has the appearance of being too heady to be practical. It is often thought to be highly theoretical or simply quixotic. That timeworn reservation has been eased somewhat by the impressive achievements of children who are given early, carefully designed opportunities to learn motor skills. Children who are exposed to circumstances that are appropriately encouraging tend to develop motor skill at a level beyond that which is normally expected. Their performances suggest that it is reasonable to hope for change in the bases for establishing expectations for skill development. Motor skill expectations probably should be set on the basis of what is possible under conditions that approach the optimal, as these conditions become known, rather than on what happens under natural or normal conditions.

The concept of optimum skill development is broad and has implications for the approach used by everyone who deals with movement; i.e., the parent, the teacher, and the coach. Each of these adults has a different role to play in the total skill development of the child, and each exerts his major influence at a particular level of development. Yet their efforts are bonded into a total influence. What is done to promote motor skill development at one level either affects or is affected by what is done to promote it at other levels. The assurance of a positive contribution from all those who participate in the promotion of basic skill development is strongly dependent upon the common possession of a broad understanding of human movement.

Everyone who works with motor skill development should have a basic knowledge of how people move. Glassow has suggested that the study of human movement should begin with an attempt to identify basic movement patterns. The point is sound because, in a sense, patterns of movement are a fundamental and significant part of the language of movement. They are descriptions of what happens whenever human movement occurs. Considering this primary relationship, preparation for promoting optimum skill development can reasonably begin with the study of certain basic motor patterns. This approach can provide an understanding of the nature of each fundamental skill which, in turn, can build into an awareness of the larger scheme of movement.

TERMINOLOGY

A brief discussion of terminology is an important preliminary to the consideration of basic movement patterns. Terminology currently used in connection with movement is a reflection of 40 years of movement pattern study. What is needed is language precise enough to differentiate and clarify but not so incisive as to provoke incessant controversy. The terminology selected for use in this book allows moderate overlapping of meanings and is reasonably liberal toward the interchangeable use of terms.

MOVEMENT. A movement is a change in position by any segment of the body. The normal anatomic segments are the parts that move, but the size of the segment can vary, especially when the arms or legs are involved. The entire arm might swing forward, the forearm might extend, or there might be flexion at the wrist. A movement by each of these segments could be contained within a single movement pattern along with other movements.

MOVEMENT PATTERN. A movement pattern is a series of movements organized in a particular time-space sequence. Movement patterns range from the almost random to the highly structured and from the simple to the complex. The meaning of the term *movement pattern* has been the subject of diverse interpretations. It is used here primarily in reference to the patterns of the basic motor skills and some narrowly defined sport skills. There are other equally useful and more expansive interpretations of the meaning of the term. It is often used to refer to an enlarged pattern formed by joining two or more fundamental skills into a continuous sequence. The fundamental skills of running and jumping are combined at the basic level as a run and jump and at the advanced level as a running high jump. A myriad of combined patterns of this sort are included in the normal motor activities of children and adults.

The term *movement pattern* is also used to refer to the common elements that appear in many skills performed in the same plane. Batting in baseball, the forehand stroke in tennis, and the sidearm throw in softball are performed at different velocities according to unique timing patterns, but in essentially the same horizontal plane with enough common elements to form a general movement pattern. The acceptance of this interpretation has been cautious but is growing because it stresses the interrelationships of basic skills and encourages an understanding of the comprehensive concept of movement. But it is important to remember that the observed similarities in movement patterns performed in the same plane are similarities in configuration and not necessarily similarities in kinematic factors, which tend to be quite specific.[5,19]

FUNDAMENTAL SKILL. A fundamental skill is a common motor activity with a general goal. It is the basis for more advanced and highly specific motor activities. Running, jumping, throwing, catching, galloping, skipping, kicking, and climbing are typical of the identifiable general motor activities included in the category of fundamental skills. Examples of attempts to present a skill hierarchy including fundamental skills can be found in the books of Schurr[22] and of Godfrey and Kephart.[10]

FUNDAMENTAL MOTOR PATTERN. A fundamental motor pattern is the general pattern of movements used in the performance of a fundamental skill. It is the composite of the common elements in the form used by skilled, mature performers. Other terms used frequently to convey essentially the same meaning are mature motor pattern, mature form, good form, basic form, and skilled form. The comprehensive meanings of these terms are not identical, but they all successfully set forth the idea of a movement pattern that is basic yet highly effective.

DEVELOPMENTAL MOTOR PATTERN. A developmental motor pattern is any movement pattern used in the performance of a fundamental skill that meets the minimal requirement for the skill but does not measure up to the mature pattern. By this definition, all developmental patterns are relatively immature patterns and involve less than skilled form. Typical developmental patterns for some of the basic skills have been identified in connection with the study of motor skill development. These unique patterns of timing and movement symbolize progress toward the achievement of mature patterns. Several special terms—unitary pattern, arm-dominated pattern, block rotation, and opening up—have been devised to describe the unique developmental motor patterns.

Unitary Pattern. A unitary pattern is one in which the movements are performed simultaneously rather than sequentially. Many of the developmental patterns in throwing, striking, and jumping tend to be unitary.

Arm-dominated Pattern. In an arm-dominated pattern, the arm(s) is the only major segment moving or is the segment initiating and leading the movement. If the primary movement is confined to the arm(s) and upper spine, the pattern is more accurately termed *top-dominated.* Throwing and striking patterns often fall into either of these two categories.

Block Rotation. Block rotation is unitary movement of the entire trunk; pelvis, spine, and shoulders rotate simultaneously. It occurs regularly in developmental throwing and striking patterns.

Opening Up. A movement pattern is opened up when there is simultaneous movement of body parts in opposite directions. This important process increases range of motion, unlocks unitary action, and contributes significantly to the development of velocity in various forms of throwing and striking.

SPORT SKILL. A sport skill is an advanced and refined version of a fundamental skill that is used in a particular way in a particular sport. The golf swing is an advanced form of striking, the running high jump is an advanced form of jumping, and the football pass is an advanced form of throwing. The presence of the fundamental motor pattern in the larger specific sport skill pattern offers visual evidence of the underlying relationship between basic and sport skills.

FORM AND PERFORMANCE. Form and performance are two well-known terms used, respectively, to describe the process and the product of movement. The relationship between them is a bit complicated and is an important one to explore because of its relevance to the concept of optimum motor skill development.

Form. Form is the process entailed in movement. "Form is a way of performing, a work method, a design of performance."[16] It includes movements, the time-space arrangement of movements, and the total visual effect produced. The relative quality of the process is indicated by the use of qualifying terms that fall somewhere in the range between good and bad, mature and immature, skilled and unskilled, effective and ineffective, or satisfactory and unsatisfactory. Positive qualifying terms imply economy of movement and conformance to effective body mechanics; negative qualifying terms indicate major departure from the compound of similarities in the form used by the highly skilled.

Performance. A performance is a motor activity that is to be done or that has been done. The term can be used acceptably to refer to the act (the child threw a ball) or to signify the outcome (a distance of 150 feet). A measured performance is not good, bad, satisfactory, or unsatisfactory in absolute terms. It is relatively good or bad depending upon the extent to which an expected outcome is achieved. A running high jump of 42 inches could be an exceptionally good jump for a child, but it would ordinarily be a mediocre jump for an adult because of the differences in the usual standards of expectation.

There is a positive but not a direct causal relationship between form and performance. Mature form enhances performance, but good performance is not totally dependent upon mature form. This side of the relationship is prominent and is emphasized when children are involved. A child who is able to use the mature form in throwing or in kicking ordinarily is not able to throw or kick as far as an adult who uses the same form. Even when two children use identical form in throwing or kicking for distance, one might throw or kick much farther than the other. In both instances the relationship between form and performance is strongly influenced by factors classified as human abilities. Strength, speed of movement, reaction time, and eye-hand coordination are among the general traits that impose limitations upon performance. Some of the abilities such as speed of movement, strength, and neuromuscular integration are particularly important factors influencing performance in tasks where the outcome is measured in terms of height, distance, or frequency. Other factors have an important bearing on accuracy of performance.

The difference in ability factors can be used to show another facet of the relationship between form and performance. An abundance of the ability factors required in a particular skill make it possible to compensate for minor violations of good form without noticeably detracting from measurable performance. Accordingly, one competitor might be able to kick or throw farther than another even though his form is not so effective. This situation is common, but it certainly is not a strong argument for accepting ineffective form. For optimum performance, all ability should be applied directly to the task rather than having part of it used to overcome minor deviations in form. It is especially important to emphasize the basic aspects of good form when the fundamental skills are being learned because, ultimately, good form is more productive of good performance than is poor form. The growing realization of this important relationship is reflected in the favorable trend toward a concern not only with what is done (performance), but also with how it is done (form). This trend augurs well for the continued growth of the large view of motor skill development.

MOTOR DEVELOPMENT

Motor development encompasses the development of the abilities that are essential to movement and the subsequent acquisition of motor skills. It may be viewed as an extensive, more or less continuous, lifelong process beginning at the prenatal stage and continuing through adult life.[13] This broad view of motor development must be kept to the fore and not allowed to slip from sight by concentrating on development at a particular stage, especially the earliest one. The motor development that ordinarily occurs in infancy and in childhood is the foundation for an almost endless process of motor skill development, yet what happens during early periods of life is only a part of the entire process. Equally important is the motor development associated with the learning of basic skills and the acquisition of advanced skills that normally follows and can occur at any age. The early part of the process or any stage of motor development can be explored in proper perspective if it is kept within the framework of the lifelong process concept.

There is a vast amount of literature describing the nature and direction of physical growth during the early years of life. The principles based upon the accumulated evidence indicate that the sequence of development is predictable and approximately the same for all children, but the rate at which specific changes take place varies from one child to another. Further, neuromuscular development follows a cephalocaudal pattern, a proximal-distal direction, and proceeds from gross to specific refinement. These broad generalities concerning physical growth and neuromuscular development help set expectations for motor skill development without tying them specifically to an age schedule.

Examples of the presence of the principles of development are scattered throughout the literature in movement studies such as the one on running and walking by Bernstein.[5] He demonstrated precisely that refinement of leg action in the two modes of locomotion proceeds in a proximal–distal direction and at a slower pace than was thought to be the case.

There is rapid physical growth during the first 2 years of life, and gross motor patterns appear. The child naturally develops the ability to perform many simple motor tasks during these years, but his development of fundamental motor skills is limited until he possesses the abilities necessary to improve his means of locomotion. Learning to walk is a signal event because it offers the infant a wider exposure to those aspects of his environment that encourage the expansion of motor behavior. The scope of his movement increases rapidly as he progresses from crawling and creeping and learns to walk. He acquires many new forms of movement, including upright patterns of locomotion and the simplest fundamental motor skills.

The early motor achievements of children have been observed and chronicled by Gesell, Bayley, Wellman, Shirley, and other pioneers in the field of motor development.[4,9,24,27] The accumulation of information has made it possible to gain insight into the natural progress that takes place as children move through various stages of development toward the achievement of mature motor patterns. The insight is limited to natural progress because it is based upon what children do under ordinary circumstances and not what they can do if given the most favorable opportunity. This is a significant qualification that applies to the bulk of the data on motor performances of children. The gap between what children do and what they can do holds an important secret to the better understanding of optimum motor development. Isolated attempts to arrange the most favorable circumstances for motor performance have produced results that strike a direct blow at the obsession with spontaneously demonstrated readiness that has been a deterrent to optimum skill development. Children seem to be capable of using certain motor patterns before they normally are asked to try them and long before the patterns appear in their motor behavior. The advantages of unusually early introduction to skills can be illustrated by the successes produced when some infants have been given the opportunity to move in the water. The early opportunity, more than the so-called swimming reflex, seems to be the really important influence on success. Considering the impact of current evidence, it is easy to conclude that the opportunities for development of fundamental skills probably are offered too late far more often than too early.

The first 5 years of life generally are regarded as a period during which the fundamental motor patterns emerge as the child deals with problems of locomotion and as he manipulates the various objects in his environment. The elementary school years have been characterized as a period of skill refinement more than a period of new skill acquisition. Typical of the research supporting this view is the work of Bernstein and Kurochkin and his associates, which indicates that the skill of walking does not truly reach adult form until puberty.[5,15]

The widely promoted general descriptions of motor skill development in childhood stress the acquisition of the basic skills and the development of mature form. They emphasize an orderly progression toward higher levels of achievement, including an introduction to sport skills. In subsequent years there is a continuation of the process toward progressively higher standards of mature performance. With a slight modification in the ultimate degree of development, the same general progression can apply to motor development at any stage of life.

MOTOR PATTERN DEVELOPMENT

There are broadly defined minimal standards for all fundamental skills. The minimal standard for running, for example, requires that the feet move forward alternately and that the push-off from the support foot be followed by a brief period of nonsupport. When this standard is met, the skill has been achieved at its barest level of proficiency. The next major goal in the development of the skill is the achievement of the standard of mature form. All movement patterns used in the performance of the skill in the interim fit into the category of developmental patterns.

Starting with a monumental study by Wild in 1937, there has been a gradual increase in the amount of available information concerning the movement patterns children use as they progress toward mature form in the fundamental skills.[29] The gradual changes in form that have been observed can be interpreted in two different ways: as developmental stages or as developmental trends.

DEVELOPMENTAL STAGES. A stage may be defined as a distinct movement pattern that commonly is present at one of the progressive levels of skill development. If the development of a particular fundamental skill is interpreted in terms of stages, the number of stages and the movement characteristics of each must be determined. These determinations have become complex rather than simple problems. A brief consideration of the use of stages in connection with throwing will serve to illustrate the problem of increased complexity. Wild observed six types of throws in the development of the mature pattern and later converted them into four stages.[29] The lack of differentiation in trunk movement in Wild's stages was noted by Hanson, who suggested refinement to clarify this aspect of the pattern.[14] Leme expanded Wild's six original types to a total of ten and gave more attention in the types to changes in the length of stride.[17] More recently, Roberton hypothesized 25 stages of throwing using only the pelvic, spinal, and arm movements in the pattern.[20] As the number of stages increased, so did the sophistication of the characteristics of each and the methods needed to identify them. Whereas Wild's four simple stages are discernible by direct observation, Roberton's profuse 25 stages can be identified only by detailed and carefully controlled film analysis. Both degrees of stage complexity are important; the former is utilitarian for the teacher, and the latter is essential for the motor development researcher.

DEVELOPMENTAL TRENDS. Improvement in some of the fundamental skills seems to be more continuous than steplike. The changes in motor patterns in these other skills are better expressed in terms of broad developmental trends than as stages. Trends are usually indicated as changes in a particular part of the movement pattern over an extended period of time. They can be described in terms of timing, range of motion, joint angles, segmental interrelationships, segmental velocities, and angular velocities.

Stages and trends are not mutually exclusive interpretations of improvement in developmental motor patterns. Both can be used satisfactorily to describe different aspects of improvement for certain skills. This becomes apparent from closer scrutiny of the function of stages. Validly defined stages are presumed to be progressive and contain patterns with distinct motor characteristics. The evidence showing precisely how an individual progresses through the different stages of the various fundamental skills is sketchy and incomplete. From what little is known, it seems that a given motor pattern could have (1) all the characteristics of a stage or (2) some of the characteristics of one stage as well as some of the characteristics of a preceding and/or succeeding stage. It also seems that pattern characteristics progress (or in some cases regress) at various rates, depending on the complexity of the fundamental skill. Thus, it appears that in some motor skills, movement characteristics progress more or less as trends while the entire motor pattern moves through designated stages.

Few longitudinal studies have been done in which the skill

development of the same children was followed for a period of several years with frequent observations. The largest portion of the information concerning the motor patterns of children is cross-sectional. It comes primarily from cinematographic and observational study of the performances of normal children at various ages. The accumulation of cross-sectional and longitudinal data suggests that stages are not steps upon which all children must tread on their way to a mature pattern, and trends are not smooth, sure progressions for all children. The type of progress seems to vary from one child to another, and the rate of progress tends to be uneven. Since these aspects of motor pattern development are imperfectly understood, it is important to continue the search for answers. Until more answers are found, what is known must not be overstated, accepted as dogma, or treated simplistically.

The preceding caution applies especially to the compulsion to transform current knowledge of motor pattern development into a form that can be used readily by the nursery or elementary school teacher. The popular approach of identifying three to five simple stages of development for each fundamental skill is not without problems. If the approach is to be practical, it must permit the teacher to assess movement patterns on the basis of easily discernible features. This requirement automatically eliminates many important characteristics of mature motor patterns because they are too fast to be seen by direct observation. The number of features lost to direct observation appears to increase with the complexity of the skill, and the difficulty of determining the simple stages that can be identified by teachers increases accordingly. In at least one instance, it has been shown that the task is not impossible. Wild took the complex skill of throwing, focused on key developmental changes, and successfully formulated four reasonably easy-to-observe stages of motor pattern development. Her stages do not encompass all the known refinements of trunk rotation and arm action in the mature form, but they allow the teacher to identify distinct critical development changes. Where such distinct changes do not exist, the use of developmental stages is unrealistic.

The exclusive use of stages to express changes in fundamental motor patterns provides a convenient and consistent approach for the teacher, but it denies possible differences in the *manner* in which the changes actually occur. For example, progress in running and in other fundamental skills seems to be more accurately described in terms of trends than in terms of stages. When that is the case, the material should be made available as trends to make it as meaningful as possible, convenience for the teacher notwithstanding. Teachers, after all, must know enough to understand the significance and limitations of simplified stages and trends, or evaluations based on their use might be misunderstood, taken too seriously, or grossly misapplied.

Knowledge of stages and trends of mature form and of the kinds of motor patterns the child might use prior to his achievement of mature form has several practical values. It establishes the identity of immature movements and patterns, assists in setting expectations for skill development, and helps in evaluating progress. The knowledge is applicable to skill development at any age; for example, stepping forward with the leg on the same side of the body as the throwing arm is a part of a typically immature throwing pattern regardless of the age of the performer. However, the significance of the same arm-same leg pattern in the throwing form of a 4-year-old child is quite different from the meaning of its presence in the form used by a 15-year-old high school sophomore. The immature movement pattern could be considered appropriate or typical at the early age level and an indication of a severe deficiency in skill development at the older age level. Mature fundamental motor patterns ought to be achieved during childhood, but there is an abundance of evidence to show that they are not.

FUNDAMENTAL MOTOR PATTERNS

Motor skill development is an extensive process during which attention is focused successively upon three major goals: (1) minimal form, (2) mature form, and (3) sport skill form. As the intermediate goal, mature form represents the culmination of early skill development and indicates the readiness to progress to advanced sports skills. The core of that central goal of skill development is the fundamental motor pattern.

A fundamental motor pattern is the underlying skeleton and the essence of what is accepted as mature form for a fundamental skill. The motor pattern for a particular skill is based upon the adept performance of the skill by adults. There are minor differences in the form used by highly skilled performers, but these are mostly stylistic variations and not important differences in the basic pattern of movements. After the minor individual variations in form have been winnowed out, the common elements that remain are the ingredients of the fundamental motor pattern. It would be a dangerous overstatement to imply that there is unanimous agreement concerning which movements to include in a fundamental pattern. The level of agreement is limited by subjective judgment in the winnowing process and by the tentative status of the knowledge of skilled performance. The degree of acceptance seems to be more uniform among those who are aware of the configurational and kinematic similarities and differences in skilled performance.

One objective method of establishing fundamental motor patterns is by the use of line diagrams that are a product of cinematographic analysis. Movement can be diagrammed by representing each body segment with a line drawn to correspond to the long axis of the segment. In Figure 5–6, the body is reduced to the skeleton of a line diagram. Each segment is shown in position during a particular phase of the movement pattern. Movements are indicated by the changes in the relationships of the lines from one phase of the pattern to another. If the skeletal diagrams of skilled performers at a corresponding point in a movement pattern are superimposed upon one another, the similarities in position become apparent as do the minor differences. The common movements in the patterns of the skilled performers can then be determined by observing changes in the superimposed diagrams at successive stages of the movement pattern. A distinct limitation in this approach is that it involves two-dimensional data. Current research techniques in biomechanics such as electrogoniometry and three-view kinematic analysis have eliminated some of the problems inherent in two-dimensional analysis and have introduced a new level of objectivity. The new techniques have produced the type and quality of information needed for greater understanding of similarities in skilled performances of a basic motor task.

SPORT SKILL PATTERNS

Sport skills are fundamental skills that have been adapted to the special requirements of a particular sport or game. The movement patterns of these skills are more precise and, for the most part, are more complex than the patterns of the basic skills. Part of the greater complexity is the use of a pattern that encompasses several fundamental skills, and part of the greater precision is the adaptation of the basic skill to the specifics of the sport.

Children routinely are allowed or encouraged to play games involving basic skills they have not had the opportunity to learn. Currently there is a stong tendency to go a step further and push children ahead into sport skills even before they have reached motor pattern development at a level remotely approaching the mature form for the underlying basic skills. When this happens, any immature movement in the pattern of the basic skill is carried forward and, at least temporarily, becomes part of the pattern used in performing the sport skill. It is well to remember also that normally there is a brief regression in the motor pattern used whenever the child moves on to a more difficult version of a skill. An excellent example of the consequences of premature initiation into the sports world was shown recently on a nationally televised program. It was purported to be a humorous story of the "losingest" team in baseball. A midget baseball team had lost all of its games by such ignominious scores as 27–2, 24–0, and 31–7. Since the opposing teams had been getting only two or three hits per game, losing apparently was due to the team's failure to hit and especially to its failure to catch. When one key member of the "losingest" team was asked for his opinion of the difficulty, he succinctly stated that everyone on the team was "chicken of the ball."

The major consequences of accelerated progression into sport skills should be considered carefully. If immature movements become a permanent part of a sport skill pattern, premature encounter with the sport is undesirable. However, if immature movements become modified positively by encouragement and the challenge of the more difficult task, the eventual result is beneficial to motor skill development. The question of when to move on to more difficult tasks is an important one with the fate of optimal motor development possibly being in the balance. Unfortunately, a patent answer to the question does not exist.

METHODOLOGY

GENERAL APPROACH TO THE COLLECTION OF DATA. It has been stated that motor development, essentially, is a study of the changes which occur in motor behavior as a result of the interaction of intrinsic and extrinsic processes. The only method of studying these changes that is fully consistent with the notion of development is the longitudinal approach.[23] It allows data to be collected on the same group of subjects for an extended period of time, which in turn provides the opportunity to determine the nature of change and to gain insight into the process(es) producing it. Longitudinal data from the Wisconsin Motor Development Center have produced some heretofore nonexistent, realistic information about intertask development. Halverson and her associates found that rotary trunk action in overarm throwing and sidearm striking developed similarly in three basic steps: (1) top-dominated rotation, (2) block rotation, and (3) pelvic-initiated rotation.[13] The Wisconsin group actually observed in a longitudinal study what might have been suspected or merely inferred from cross-sectional data.

Because of the difficulties inherent in the collection of longitudinal data, a cross-sectional approach has been used in the overwhelming bulk of motor development research. By collecting data on subjects at different age levels, it has been possible to piece together a reasonably acceptable picture of the process of motor skill development, insofar as the process is reflected in successive age group behavior. The picture of motor pattern changes resulting from cross-sectional studies seems to be supported by the data on changes from a limited number of longitudinal investigations. The vital difference between the two methods is that only the longitudinal approach can reveal the process of development in its truest sense, that is, as it occurs in a given individual. Both methods are and have been valuable in the study of motor development, but the critical need now is for the more extensive collection of longitudinal data.

Equipment and Procedure. The concept of motor development being a lifelong process requires the collection of data on motor behavior at all ages. It is important to collect the most valid and accurate data possible, and efforts toward this goal are being intensified. The type of data that can be collected varies with the sophistication of the equipment available and the design of the method for collecting it. There are practical limits on both equipment and design when young children are being studied. Preschool children, especially during infancy, tend to be difficult subjects unless special procedures are followed. Because testing situations are unnatural for most children, they are inclined to be somewhat apprehensive, inattentive, sporadic, or uncooperative. Halverson and her colleagues have improved the process of data collection vastly by providing generous prefilming orientation to put the child at ease. Only when children are free to move in a way that is natural for them, is it possible to acquire realistic information relative to the way they can move.

The specific information about movement generally sought includes a description of (1) the movements in a pattern, (2) the range of motion at each active joint, (3) the angular velocities accompanying segmental movement, (4) the timing of movement sequences, (5) the amount of time devoted to each phase of a pattern, and (6) projection angles and velocities. One-, two-, or three-view film analysis is the major source of the desired information.[2,21,25] Filming is preceded by careful preparation and planning and is done under highly controlled conditions. The segments of the performer's body are marked for clear identification, the distance between the subject and the camera is predetermined, and background reference points are established. If several cameras are used for simultaneous filming from different views, a coordinating device is included. Despite the controls in the procedure, there are three well-known limitations of cinematographic analysis: the accuracy of the measurements, the quality of the form used by the subjects, and variability in the effort put forth by the performer. All of these factors must be considered in assessing the actual value of a film analysis. The limitations in measurement are due to factors such as distortion caused by camera angles, exceptional speed during movement, movement in three dimensions, and accuracy of the subject's reference marks. Some of these limitations can be minimized by the use of recently developed complex procedures.[1]

The second limitation is a problem of a different order and must receive careful attention when mature or skilled form is being determined. An analysis of a skill, regardless of the precision of the measurement, is no better than the form of the performer whose movement was studied. The usual procedure when attempting to determine good form is to use the best performer available as a subject. The subjects in reported cinematographic studies vary from international champions, to varsity athletes, instructors, graduate students, and simply the best students in a class. Thus, the quality of the information from film studies can vary considerably, and the value will vary accordingly. Closely related to the question of the quality of the subject's form is the possible problem of variation in the intensity of his effort during performance. Since maximum controlled velocity is required to produce mature patterns in running, jumping, throwing, striking, and kicking, it is essential that these skills be performed with full effort or the true quality of a subject's performance cannot be determined. Waterland has shown that motor patterns can vary when the intensity of the effort put forth is significantly reduced.[26] It is obvious that developmental patterns can be distorted if the child being filmed tries either too hard or not hard enough. The velocity factor is a serious problem for those studying motor development because it can act in several ways to produce misleading results in motor behavior analysis.[28]

With increasing frequency, cinematography and electrogoniometry are combined in the kinematic and configurational analysis of motor behavior. However, the latter method can also be used independently. Electrogoniometry is an objective and reliable procedure in which elgons are attached to the limbs being studied and direct measurement of action at the joints is made during movement. The electrogoniometer requires complicated recording instruments and is somewhat of a hindrance to movement, but it provides faster and more accurate measurement of movement at many joints than is possible with film analysis.

A useful but less direct source of information concerning status or changes in movement patterns is electromyographic data.[3] Electrodes are attached to the body to pick up the action potentials of the muscles involved in movement. In this way, electromyography serves more as an adjunct to the other methods than as a primary source of information in movement analysis. It does not show movement patterns so precisely as in cinematography or electrogoniometry but can provide evidence of movement pattern maturation in terms of changes from unitary to sequential patterning and in the reduction of nonproductive muscular involvement.[7] The major drawback to the use of electromyographic technique in the study of velocity-oriented movement is that the information it provides becomes less dependable as the speed of movement increases.

There is a trend toward the use of multiple-data systems involving various combinations of cinematography, electrogoniometry, electromyography, along with force platforms and other sophisticated equipment to study movement. Despite the refinement in research technique and design, it is paradoxical that the scope of controversy relative to what is correct in certain skills merely enlarges. The divergent findings from research on the biomechanics of running presented in the recent summary by Dillman are a prime example.[8]

MOVEMENT AND MECHANICS

Good form and effective motor patterns characteristically are consistent with the laws of mechanics. Recognition of this simple truth has resulted in the formulation of principles based upon physical laws. In turn, the established mechanical principles have become an indispensable basis for understanding why movement, form, and performance are effective or ineffective. The principles are useful in the evaluation of skill descriptions and in the interpretation of the meaning of developmental trends, developmental patterns, and individual performance. Full treatment of the mechanics of movement is far beyond the scope of this presentation; however, it is necessary that anyone who is interested in motor skill development be introduced to a few principles that apply to most of the fundamental motor patterns.

Selected Mechanical Principles

1. *Force must be applied to change the velocity of a body.* This principle based on Newton's first law is a logical one to begin with because it applies to all human movement. In order to be able to use effective form there must be sufficient force available to

start, accelerate, stop, or change direction of movement according to the prescribed pattern. The primary source of force in the human body is physical strength applied in the form of muscular contraction. Ordinarily, adults have sufficient strength for mature motor patterns so that lack of strength is not so much a limitation on form for them as it is a restriction on maximum performance. With children, lack of strength often is a definite limiting factor in both form and maximum performance. During his early development, the child's movement patterns are closely related to the amount of force he has available.

2. *Linear and angular motion must be integrated for optimal performance in many movement patterns.* When a pattern includes both forward and turning movements, they must be combined without loss of the benefits of either. The linear and the angular movements in a pattern contribute significantly both to the final application of force and to the resultant direction of the movement. Mature patterns of throwing, striking, and kicking, for example, are initiated by a forward step, followed in quick succession by a series of angular movements that provide body rotation. Correct timing in the combination of the step and the turn in these skills produces the desired continuity of motion and resulting optimal performance.

3. *When several forces are applied in succession, each succeeding force must be applied at the point when the preceding one has made its greatest contribution in imparting velocity.* This principle is one expression of the effective timing of movements in a skill pattern. It is especially important because movements in mature motor patterns tend to occur sequentially rather than simultaneously. Each new movement in a motor pattern should be added after the force that produced the preceding one has made its most effective contribution, i.e., when it no longer contributes directly to acceleration. In mature movement patterns, the movements normally are arranged in terms of the amount of velocity each contributes to the total movement with the strongest but slowest force acting first and the weakest but fastest force last. This biomechanical principle comes into operation increasingly as a child moves from a unitary to a sequential pattern in a fundamental skill.

4. *Additional linear and angular velocity may be gained by increasing the distance over which force is applied.* The resultant or final velocity of a movement can be increased by providing additional distance over which to accelerate. Minor adjustments often provide the additional distance without detracting from the effectiveness of the basic pattern. Linear velocity can be increased by lengthening the run before the long jump or by

stepping forward with the ball before throwing it. Turning the body before making a throw, pivoting with a backswing before the tennis stroke, and cocking the lower leg backward before the kick are aspects of form specifically calculated to provide additional distance over which to gain angular velocity. This principle is not without practical limitations. Additional distance over which to accelerate is valuable only insofar as its contribution is positive. If a batter cocked his body too far, he would not be able to see the ball coming toward him nor would he have time to swing the bat all the way around to the striking area.

5. *The potential linear velocity at the end of a lever is increased by increasing the length of the lever.* When angular velocity remains constant, the longer the lever, the greater is the linear velocity at its end. Mature movement patterns utilize the principle of the long lever particularly when linear velocity contributes to the force imparted to an object as in striking, kicking, and throwing. The arms used in the striking motion are relatively straight at the moment of impact, the kicking leg is approximately straight at the knee at the time of contact, and the throwing arm is nearly extended at the elbow when the ball is released. A significant problem in the utilization of this principle is the fact that a long lever offers more reaction and is more difficult to move than a short lever. However, the difficulty can be overcome by keeping the lever short during the early part of a movement until momentum can be developed. In the latter phase of the pattern, the lever can be lengthened to the performer's advantage by applying available force, or it may be lengthened spontaneously if the pattern and velocity of the early movements produce a whipping action. Either of these lever-lengthening procedures may be used in the extension of the lower leg in the kick or in the extension of the forearm in the throw, depending upon the intended velocity of the movements.

6. *For every action there is a reaction which is equal in amount and opposite in direction.* This principle is based upon Newton's third law and refers to both linear and angular motion. In application, the principle requires that adjustments be made to sustain the value of the primary forces in any movement pattern. Every skillful performer accounts for the phenomenon of reaction in identifiable ways. One of the common adjustments to angular action is the opposition used in vigorous running; as one leg is swung forward, the arm on the opposite side of the body also is swung forward in reaction. In like manner, body segments are moved in various and complex ways to counterbalance the action of other segments so the productive flow of energy in the movement pattern is preserved. Although reaction must always

be accounted for in movement, its effect is particularly notice-able and problematic when the performer is airborne. Accord-ingly, mature movement patterns provide for the most forceful movements to be made while there is contact with the ground, and body levers which are as long and as massive as possible are created to deal with the inevitable reactions to movements while airborne. These adaptations are quite apparent in long jumping and in diving.

7. *The final direction of a moving body is a resultant of the magnitude and direction of all the forces which have been applied.* Knowledge of this principle is helpful in understanding ballistic and sustained human movements as well as the flight of objects which have been thrown, struck, or kicked. Manipulation of the movements in a pattern is the means by which the resultant direction of the motion is controlled. If the objective of a particular movement pattern is a vertical jump, the forces must be predominantly vertical to produce the desired direction at takeoff. On the other hand, if the objective of the pattern is a long jump, vertical forces must be minimized and horizontal forces emphasized for a low forward takeoff angle. By observing the outcome of a performance, the effectiveness of the application of forces can be determined and adjustments made accordingly.

The selected mechanical principles included in this brief introduction are much like common threads running through the fabric of effective movement. Most of them are applicable to some degree in all of the fundamental motor patterns. For quick reference, the major principles that apply to each pattern are summarized in the respective chapters.

WORKING KNOWLEDGE AND MOTOR SKILL DEVELOPMENT

Motor skill development is directly influenced by the quality and the quantity of the working knowledge of those who labor to promote it. Working knowledge is more than what one knows about what he is doing; it is what one uses of what he knows. Those who are intimately involved with skill development can improve their effectiveness by keeping pace with current facts and by translating new information into action. This process requires the combined efforts of those who provide the new information and those who use it.

The responsibility for conducting formal research on motor behavior falls to the specialist who has the time, the skills, and the equipment necessary to do the job properly. Every adult who works directly with some phase of motor development has the equally important responsibility of trying to put new information into practice. However, the fruit of research must be evaluated critically before being collated into working knowledge. The good intention of translating the results of research into a form that can be used by the practitioner occasionally can misfire or be misdirected. An example will serve as a caution. A striking task was devised and administered to 600 first, third, and fifth grade boys and girls.[18] The task required the child to stand 5 feet in front of and 10 feet to the left of a piece of apparatus that rolled an 8-inch playground ball out of an opening 12 feet from the floor. After the ball struck the floor, the child was to move and try to strike the ball in a forward direction using a paddle ball racket. The conclusion from the analysis of data was that the task was an appropriate instructional activity at the first grade level but was too easy for third and fifth grade children. This finding was translated into the following practical recommendation: "Teachers must remember one important point, when teaching children to hit a ball with a bat or racket, the ball should be allowed to bounce before it is struck." The recommendation seems ill-founded for more than one reason. The first reason is the presumed causal relationship between the bounce and the amount of success in the task. The high degree of success achieved undoubtedly was due partly to the incongruous combination of equipment; i.e., 8-inch diameter ball and short-handled racket. Also, both the immature overhand swing shown in the illustrations of the task and the slow and predictable movement of the ball after it bounced must have contributed significantly to the widespread success. Another reason for questioning the validity of the recommendation is common experience to the contrary which has been supported by documented findings. The longitudinal data of Halverson and Roberton showed that "the children could not successfully contact a bouncing ball with a sidearm pattern at the same age as success with the aerial ball was possible."[12]

Every professional who works with children on a daily basis is his own quality control expert because he must decide which information and recommendations are believable and useful. Ideally his working knowledge should be kept in a state of flux. That dynamic condition is possible if he questions traditional ideas and facts, seeks and carefully appraises new information, and discards barren knowledge.

BIBLIOGRAPHY

1. Adrian, M.: Cinematographic, electromyographic, and electrogoniometric techniques for analyzing human movements. *In* Exercise and Sport Sciences Reviews, Vol. I (Wilmore, ed.). New York, Academic Press, 1973.

2. Atwater, A.: Cinematographic analyses of human movement. *In* Exercise and Sport Sciences Reviews, Vol. I (Wilmore, ed.). New York, Academic Press, 1973.
3. Basmajian, J.: Electromyographic analyses of basic movement patterns. *In* Exercise and Sport Sciences Reviews, Vol. I (Wilmore, ed.). New York, Academic Press, 1973.
4. Bayley, N.: The development of motor abilities during the first three years. Monogr. Soc. Res. Child Dev., *1*:1, 1935.
5. Bernstein, N. A.: The Coordination and Regulation of Movements. Oxford, Pergamon Press, 1967.
6. Cooper, J., and Glassow, R.: Kinesiology. St. Louis, C. V. Mosby Co., 1972.
7. Deutsch, H.: Kinesiological implications of electromyography. *In* Biomechanics (Cooper, ed.). Chicago, The Athletic Institute, 1971.
8. Dillman, C. J.: Kinematic analyses of running. *In* Exercise and Sport Sciences Reviews, Vol. III (Wilmore and Keogh, eds.). New York, Academic Press, 1975.
9. Gesell, A.: The First Five Years of Life. New York, Harper and Brothers, 1940.
10. Godfrey, B. B., and Kephart, N. C.: Movement Patterns and Motor Education. New York, Appleton-Century-Crofts, 1969.
11. Halverson, L. E.: Development of motor patterns in young children. Quest, *6*:44, 1966.
12. Halverson, L. E., and Roberton, M. A.: A Study of Motor Pattern Development in Young Children. Report to the National Convention of AAHPER, Chicago, 1966.
13. Halverson, L. E., Roberton, M. A., and Harper, C.: Current research in motor development. J. Res. Dev. Educ., *6*:3, 1973.
14. Hanson, S. A.: A Comparison of the Overhand Throw Performance of Instructed and Non-Instructed Kindergarten Boys and Girls. Unpublished Master's Thesis, University of Wisconsin, 1961.
15. Kurochkin, Y. V., Alyakin, L. N., and Sinitzky, Y. F.: Characterization of walking of children by data of podography and electrogoniometry. Ortop. Travmatol. Protez., *35*:44, 1974.
16. Lawther, J.: Directing motor skill learning. Quest, *6*:68, 1966.
17. Leme, S.: Developmental Throwing Patterns in Adult Female Performers Within a Selected Velocity Range. Unpublished Master's Thesis, University of Wisconsin, 1973.
18. Pederson, E.: A Study of Ball Catching Abilities of First-, Third-, and Fifth-Grade Children on Twelve Selected Ball Catching Tasks. Unpublished Doctoral Dissertation, Indiana University, 1973.
19. Poe, A.: A Description of the Movement Characteristics of Two-Year-Old Children Performing the Jump and Reach. Unpublished Master's Thesis, University of Wisconsin, 1973.
20. Roberton, M. A.: Stability of Stage Categorizations Across Trials: Implications for the 'Stage Theory' of Overarm Throw Development. Unpublished Doctoral Dissertation, University of Wisconsin, 1975.
21. Roberts, E. M.: Cinematography in biomechanical investigation. *In* Biomechanics (Cooper, ed.). Chicago, The Athletic Institute, 1971.
22. Schurr, E.: Movement Experiences for Children: A Humanistic Approach to Elementary School Physical Education. Englewood Cliffs, N. J., Prentice-Hall, Inc., 1975.
23. Seefeldt, V.: A researchers view: Motor development. Elementary School Physical Education: Progress—Problems—Predictions. The Women's Physical Education Alumnae Association, University of Wisconsin, 1974.
24. Shirley, M. M.: The First Two Years: A Study of Twenty-Five Babies, Vol. 1. Minneapolis, University of Minnesota Press, 1931.
25. Taylor, P. R.: Essentials in cinematographical research. *In* Biomechanics (Cooper, ed.). Chicago, The Athletic Institute, 1971.
26. Waterland, J. C.: Integration of movement. *In* Medicine and Sport, Vol. 2: Biomechanics (Wartenweiler, Jokl, and Hebbelinck, eds.). Baltimore, University Park Press, 1968.

27. Wellman, B.: Motor achievements of preschool children. Childhood Educ., *13*:311, 1937.
28. Wickstrom, R.: Developmental kinesiology. *In* Exercise and Sport Sciences Reviews, Vol. III (Wilmore and Keogh, eds.). New York, Academic Press, 1975.
29. Wild, M.: The behavior pattern of throwing and some observations concerning its course of development in children. Res. Q. Am. Assoc. Health Phys. Educ., *9*(3):20, 1938.

2

WALKING

Walking is a natural form of upright locomotion. Its motor pattern is distinguished by progressive alternate leg action and continuous contact with the supporting surface. A full cycle in the motor pattern consists of a swing phase and a stance or support phase for each leg. As the swing leg moves forward it regains contact with a heel-strike before the toes of the support foot break contact with the supporting surface. Momentary double support occurs because normal walking is done at a slow to moderately fast pace rather than at maximum locomotor velocity as in speed-walking or running. Heel-toe speed-walking is a special track and field athletics event requiring an awkward, rather grotesque technique quite unlike the smooth graceful pattern of natural walking, and running breaks heel-toe continuity by having periods of nonsupport.

PREWALKING-WALKING PROGRESSION

Nearly half a century ago Shirley referred to walking as the most spectacular and probably the most important single phase of motor development.[12] Her evaluation of the relative importance of walking might seem a bit overdrawn today, but it helped establish the acquisition of upright bipedal locomotion as a prime developmental event. Until the child can walk independently, his environment with its potential for motor experience is severely limited.

The rate at which a child develops the ability to walk is controlled by his own rate of maturation. He cannot move independently in the upright position until he has developed sufficient muscular strength, adequate antigravity reflexes, and minimally effective balance mechanisms. He cannot walk efficiently and effectively until his nervous system is capable of properly controlling his muscular coordination. As the developmental process proceeds, the child progresses from crawling, to creeping, to cruising or hitching, and finally to walking. The process is orderly but typically involves minor regressions as noted in Gesell's system of reciprocal interweaving.[4] The extent of individual differences in the age at which each of the prewalking milestones might be reached is illustrated in data presented by Burnett and Johnson.[2] The averages and ranges were as follows: crawling—7 months (4½ to 9½), creeping—8½ months (5 to 14½), cruising—10 months (7 to 11½), and independent walking—12½ months (9 to 17).

The prewalking–walking progressions of 20 infants were studied in detail for a period of 2 years by Shirley.[12] She found that nearly every baby passed through four distinct stages of development in the walking process.

STAGE I. The infant makes dancing and patting steps against the floor from a supported position. He neither stiffens his knees nor supports his weight.

STAGE II. The infant stands with support. He uses his feet for weight bearing and his outstretched arms (which are held) for balance.

STAGE III. The infant walks when led by both hands.

STAGE IV. The infant walks alone.

The four stages are easily identified but can be misunderstood if they are not interpreted in the proper context. Shirley obviously confined her stages to progress in the upright position and did not intend to include sequential changes in the total development of locomotion. If locomotor developments in the horizontal position had not been excluded, it could be seen that most infants reach stages I and II in the walking process described by Shirley before they are able to creep.

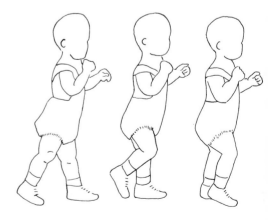

FIG. 2–1. The unsteady walking pattern of a 14½-month-old girl 7 days after taking her first unsupported steps. She shows "high guard" arm position, flat-footed contact, and single-knee-lock leg action.

MOTOR PATTERNS IN THE DEVELOPMENT OF WALKING

Initial attempts at independent walking are precarious adventures. Balance is lost easily, falls are common, but progress is rapid. Once the child is able to take a few controlled steps, his progress in walking proceeds at an exponential rate, at least in terms of the number of continuous steps taken.[11] Rapid progress is manifested, too, by the many improvements in his movement pattern.

The initial patterns used in independent walking clearly demonstrate that all neophyte walkers experience difficulty in maintaining dynamic balance, especially lateral dynamic stability, during the swing phase of the pattern. The rigid, halting initial pattern is characterized by short steps, flat-footed contact, outtoeing foot angle (heel-toe angle from line of progression), wide dynamic base (distance of each heel from center line during double stance), flexed knee at contact with quick knee extension, little purposeful ankle movement, excessive hip flexion and limited hip extension, slight pelvic tilt (drop of pelvis away from support side), no pelvic rotation (forward-backward movement around the vertical axis), forward trunk inclination, and arms fixed in sideward elevation with half-flexed elbows (Fig. 2–1).

Improvement in each feature of the pattern is more gradual than abrupt, and the rate of improvement varies from one feature to another. The changes are notably consistent with the cephalocaudal course of nervous system development. To illustrate, the average ages at which various gait characteristics appeared in the patterns of the 28 children studied by Burnett and Johnson were as follows: pelvic tilt, 13.4 months; pelvic rotation, 13.8 months; flexion midstance, 16.3 months; feet-within-trunk-width base, 17.0 months; synchronous arm move-

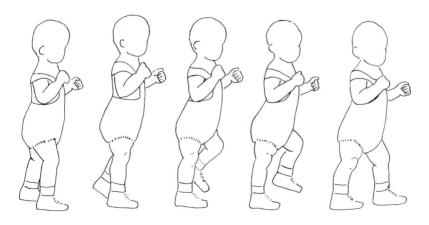

ment, 18.0 months; heel-strike, 18.5 months; mature foot and knee mechanism, 19.5 months.[2]

Since development toward the mature pattern of walking does not seem to occur as definite steps or characteristic stages, the development for each major feature of the pattern will be traced briefly in terms of its general trend.

Step Length

The length of the stride is extended by small annual increments. The magnitude of the changes is typified by Scrutton's data based on heel-to-heel measurements of 97 children.[10] Average length of stride increased from 10 inches at age 1 year, to 11.5 inches at age 2 years, to 13.0 inches at age 3 years, to 15.0 inches at age 4 years. The consistency of stride length improves for each leg, and the length of stride for right and left legs becomes increasingly more similar.

Foot Contact

Flat-footed contact is the norm for beginning unsupported walkers with a few infants starting as "toe steppers." Progress in this feature of the pattern is unusually slow, but changes in the entire foot-knee mechanism gradually lead to heel-strike at contact.

Dynamic Base

Foot placement is relatively wide for most infants when they take their first independent steps (Fig. 2–2). The dynamic base narrows rather promptly and soon falls within the lateral dimensions of the trunk, thereafter continuing medialward toward the line of progression. After the initial rapid improvement, there is only a slight tendency for dynamic base to narrow

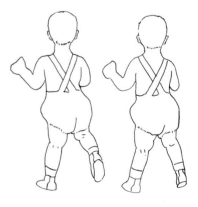

FIG. 2–2. Lateral stability in the initial phase of independent walking is provided by a dynamic base greater than trunk width.

during childhood. Scrutton concluded that this feature of the pattern changes very little in the age range of 13 months to 4 years 11 months which he had studied.[10]

Foot Angle

The initial degree of outtoeing is reduced somewhat but stabilizes and remains fairly uniform with advancing age. Intoeing gaits are considered to be abnormal.[3]

Hip Excursion

The infantile pattern stresses flexion and minimizes extension at the hip. There are a gradual decrease in maximum hip flexion during the swing phase and an increase in maximum hip extension at the end of stance. The latter change was mentioned by Statham and Murray as the main mechanism involved at the developmental level when increased skill produced longer strides.[13] The large amount of hip flexion at the end of the leg swing sometimes gives the appearance of "high stepping" without actually producing excessive foot clearance.

Knee-Ankle Mechanism

The changes in the function of this aspect of the walking pattern are undoubtedly the most vital to progress toward the mature form. In beginning form, flat-footed contact with the knee in flexion is followed by extension at the knee and passive flexion at the ankle during stance. Little by little that pattern is changed to an extension-flexion-extension form. There is a trend toward achieving the "double knee lock" form which involves heel-strike with knee in extension, immediate plantar flexion of the foot and knee flexion until near midstance, and knee extension and heel raise just prior to the swing phase. The

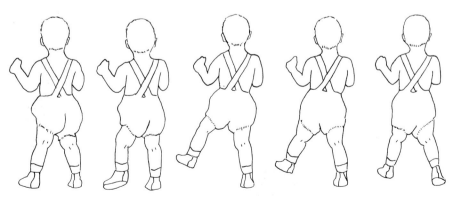

FIG. 2–3. Slow walking pace for a 16-month-old boy. There is bare evidence of heel-strike, and arm swing is minimal.

extension-flexion-extension change is smooth and allows the weight of the body to roll across the foot, from heel to toe.

Pelvic Tilt

There usually is a trace of pelvic tilt at the onset of independent walking. The tilt increases slightly as walking improves.

Pelvic Rotation

Ordinarily pelvic rotation appears after unsupported walking begins and slowly becomes part of the pattern. Its progress is related to the rate of maturation of leg action in the pattern.

Trunk Inclination

The slight forward inclination of the trunk and accompanying downward tilt of the pelvis of the initial pattern of walking become less pronounced as balance improves and as walking becomes more controlled.

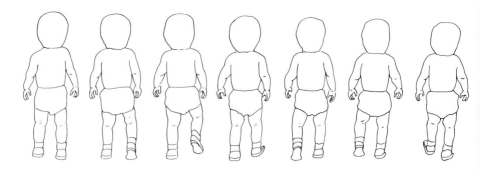

FIG. 2–4. Dynamic base narrows quickly and heel-strike is usually present in walking form by age 2 years.

Arm Action

The arms become unlocked from the abducted, elbow-flexed position and are gradually lowered and held at the side of the body (Fig. 2–3). This change in arm position frequently accompanies the narrowing of the dynamic base (Fig. 2–4). Once lowered, the arms begin to swing. The swing might be confined initially to flexion at the elbow during contralateral leg swing.[2] Eventually the arms reach the point where they swing reflexly in opposition to leg action.

EVALUATION OF PROGRESS IN WALKING

Walking is an extremely complex skill. Adult form for the skill might not be achieved until as late as mid-adolescence, depending upon the criteria used for the evaluation of progress.[1,7] The most elementary and widely utilitarian method is careful observation of the configuration of the pattern the child uses in walking, and a feature-by-feature comparison of that pattern with the model of adult form. These comparisons show that a child typically progresses to the point where his pattern of walking barely demonstrates the presence of all the elements in mature gait, including proper knee-foot action and arm swing. Most children have reached this level by 2 years of age, and there continues to be detectable improvement in rhythm and coordination for another 2 to 3 years. When the child is 4 or 5 years old, most of the utility of the observation method is lost. Subtle refinements in the configuration of the patterns are difficult to discern in children beyond the preschool ages. However, it has been demonstrated in several ways that improvement in walking actually does continue for several years.

Okamoto used electromyography to study progress in walking skill.[8] He measured progress in terms of changes in the functional mechanism of the muscles used. Infants, without exception, used their muscles inefficiently. They timed contractions improperly and used muscles that did not contribute directly to the movement pattern as they began to walk without support. Characteristics of the infantile pattern were disappearing at the end of the second year, and the adult form of leg action was being acquired. From that time on, the discharge patterns of the muscles involved in many of the movement characteristics began to show similarities to the adult pattern. Based on his electromyographic data, Okamoto concluded that "the period around the third year is the most important for the transition to the adult pattern."[8] He found partial contractions of unnecessary muscles until the sixth year, but most had disappeared, and the discharge patterns after the seventh year were almost similar to those of the adult.

Progress in walking can also be evaluated by measuring changes in the magnitude and the timing of movements in the pattern. Grieve and Gear verified that the very young child shows no consistency of timing in his walking pattern and is unpredictable in the way in which he changes speed.[5] One consistent aspect found in the young child's immature walking behavior was a positive relationship between the time of swing and length of stride. Progress can be measured in terms of this feature. Grieve and Gear traced the progression of change from a positive relationship between the time of swing and the relative speed of walking, through a reversal to a negative regression between the time of swing and the relative speed. Gradual changes of this sort cannot be observed directly but must be the result of careful measurement and calculation. Another change that must be measured rather than observed visually is the decrease in the proportion of time spent in stance. Because of the characteristic period of double support, the percentage of time in

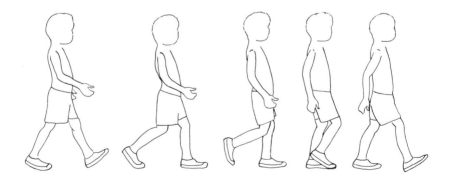

FIG. 2–5. A 50-month-old boy uses heel-strike and "double knee lock" when walking, but he swings his arms unevenly (virtually no movement with left arm).

the whole walking cycle spent in stance remains larger than in swing, but the relative amount becomes progressively less.

Of the available ways to evaluate progress in the skill of walking, the only obviously practical one is direct visual observation of changes in the conformation of the pattern (Fig. 2–5). For most requirements, it is quite satisfactory. However, direct visual observation cannot show the kinematics of progress, nor can it provide the underlying evidence necessary for valid comparisons with adult form.

MATURE PATTERN OF WALKING

In the adult pattern of walking, the weight of the body is supported alternately by right and left legs with both legs contributing support during the transitional phases (Figs. 2–6; 2–7). There is a smooth cycle of alternating single and double leg supports as the body is moved forward. The rhythmical shifting of support from right leg, to both legs, to left leg, and back to both legs produces three-dimensional movement of the walker's center of gravity. While his center of gravity is moving forward, it is simultaneously moving upward or downward and toward one side or the other, depending upon which is the primary support side. If the gait is normal and the pace is moderate, the total vertical displacement for a full cycle in the average adult pattern is less than 2 inches, and the total lateral displacement is approximately the same.[9] The following movements contribute to the effective control of the displacement of the center of gravity of the body during walking and are the essential features of the adult pattern.

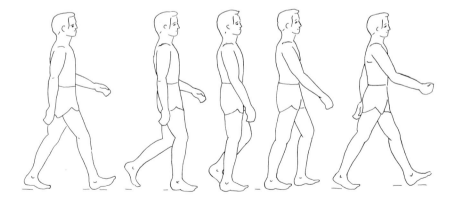

FIG. 2–6. Mature pattern of walking—lateral view. Key features are heel-strike, "double knee lock," and coordinated arm swing.

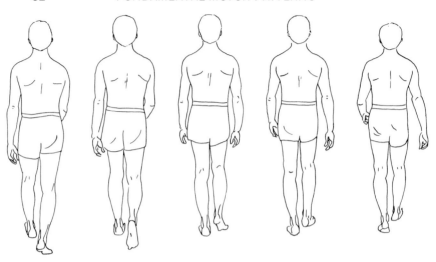

FIG. 2–7. Mature pattern of walking—posterior view. Dynamic base is narrow and arm opposition is reflex-controlled.

1. The swing leg is straight at the knee, and the foot is at approximately a right angle with the lower leg at heel-strike.
2. Extension at the hip, flexion at the knee, and plantar-flexion of the foot begin immediately after heel-strike and continue briefly until there is full sole contact. The swing leg flexes and moves forward.
3. Knee and foot action reverse to extension and dorsiflexion, respectively, and extension at the hip continues.
4. The heel of the swing leg contacts the supporting surface as the heel of the support leg leaves it (double support phase of stance).
5. The pelvis shifts laterally toward the support leg and tilts downward on the swing side in the stance phase.
6. The arms swing reflexly in opposition to leg movement.

Action of Leg During Stance

A leg is in the stance phase of the walking cycle from the instant of heel-strike until the moment of toe lift. While in stance it proceeds through the "double knee lock" sequence which helps control the peak of the arc of the movement of the center of gravity and also helps maintain continuity of forward motion. At heel-strike, the hip is moderately flexed, the knee is straight, and the ankle is in a neutral position. Immediately after heel-strike, the foot begins to plantar-flex, and the knee begins to flex. This action is continued for the brief time it takes for the foot to come into full contact with the supporting surface. Then reversal begins with dorsiflexion of the foot and extension at the knee. There is extension at the hip during the early period and throughout most of the stance phase. About two-thirds of the way through the support phase, the heel begins to rise from the contacting surface, and almost immediately the swing leg enters stance. The back support leg then makes its final contribution to forward motion with a foot push as the leg is flexing both at hip and at knee.

Action of Leg During Swing

In the transition from the stance to the swing phase, all adult lower limb patterns are characterized by a stereotyped sequence in reversal in direction of rotation, with the knee flexing first, the hip second, and the ankle last.[13] This particular sequence of movements, along with a small amount of toe elevation in the early part of the swing phase, contributes to the ease of clearance. When the walking surface has been cleared by the foot of the swing leg, flexion at the ankle ceases, and action at the knee undergoes reversal from flexion to extension. Extension at the knee after the midpoint of the forward swing allows the foot to be brought into the heel-strike position with a minimum of flexion at the hip.

Pelvic Rotation and Pelvic Tilt

The pelvis rotates backward on the side of the support leg and forward on the side of the swing leg. Rotation of the pelvis around the long axis of the body increases with the length of the stride. At the same time the pelvis is rotating, it is shifting laterally toward the support leg and is tilting downward on the side of the swing leg. Both lateral shift and lateral tilt increase in amount until midstance and then smoothly reverse the process. These two adjustments in pelvic motion minimize displacement of the center of gravity in the frontal plane during walking.

Action of Arms

Arms remain in natural extension at the elbow and swing reflexly in opposition to leg action. The direction of arm swing is slightly medialward, but it continues to be basically in the anteroposterior plane. There is approximately twice as much forward as backward excursion of the arms from the resting position during normal walking pace. The range of arm motion increases with increased pace, and the arms begin to bend at the elbows near the upper limit of walking speed.

The configuration of the adult pattern of walking shows

smoothness, rhythm, and uniformity, but under the conformation, the adult pattern lacks perfection as is the case with all mature motor skill patterns. Ismail used a force platform to analyze the walking patterns of a group of adult males who had normal gaits.[6] He discovered that the force traces for the right and the left foot for a given individual are not identical and concluded that in adult normal gait one foot is favored over the other. Apparently this minor deviation from uniform force production does not adversely affect the normality or effectiveness of adult gait. Presumably there are other minor deviations in normal gait that are similarly benign.

MECHANICAL PRINCIPLES APPLICABLE TO WALKING

Many of the mechanical principles that apply to walking are more specialized and complex than the simple principles included in Chapter 1. However, two of these are important and relevant.

1. Force must be applied to change the velocity of a body (overcome inertia and initiate forward movement).
2. For every action there is a reaction which is equal in amount and opposite in direction (opposition of arm and leg movement).

BIBLIOGRAPHY

1. Bernstein, N. A.: The Coordination and Regulation of Movements. Oxford, Pergamon Press, 1967.
2. Burnett, C. N., and Johnson, E. W.: Development of gait in childhood, Part II. Dev. Med. Child Neurol., *13*:207, 1971.
3. Engel, G. M., and Staheli, L. T.: The natural history of torsion and other factors influencing gait in childhood. Clin. Orthop., *99*:12, 1974.
4. Gesell, A.: The ontogenesis of infant behavior. *In* Manual of Child Psychology (Carmichael, ed.). New York, Wiley, 1954.
5. Grieve, D. W., and Gear, R. J.: The relationship between length of stride, step frequency, time of swing and speed of walking for children and adults. Ergonomics, *9*:379, 1966.
6. Ismail, A. H.: Analysis of normal gaits utilizing a special force platform. *In* Medicine and Sport, Vol. 2: Biomechanics (Wartenweiler, Jokl, and Hebbelinck, eds.). Baltimore, University Park Press, 1968.
7. Kurochkin, Y. V., Alyakin, L. N., and Sinitzky, Y. F.: Characterization of walking of children by data of podography and electrogoniometry. Ortop. Travmatol. Protez., *35*:44, 1974.
8. Okamoto, T.: Electromyographic study of the learning process of walking in 1- and 2-year-old infants. *In* Medicine and Sport, Vol. 8: Biomechanics III (Jokl, ed.). Basel, Karger, 1973.
9. Saunders, J. B., Inman, V. T., and Eberhart, H. D.: The major determinants in normal and pathological gait. J. Bone Joint Surg., *35-A*:543, 1953.
10. Scrutton, D. S.: Footprint sequences of normal children under five years old. Dev. Med. Child Neurol., *11*:44, 1969.
11. Shapiro, H.: The development of walking in a child. J. Genet. Psychol., *100*:221, 1962.

12. Shirley, M. M.: The First Two Years: A Study of Twenty-Five Babies, Vol. 1, Postural and Locomotor Development. Minneapolis, University of Minnesota Press, 1931.
13. Statham, L. and Murray, M. P.: Early walking patterns of normal children. Clin. Orthop., *79*:8, 1971.

3

RUNNING

Running is an exaggerated form and a natural extension of the basic skill of walking. In the mature pattern of walking, one foot moves ahead of the other with the heel of the forward foot touching the ground before the toe of the opposite foot pushes off, and the arms and legs move synchronously in opposition. The distinguishing factor in running is a phase in which the body is propelled through space with no support from either leg. As defined by Slocum and James, "Running is really a series of smoothly coordinated jumps during which the body weight is borne on one foot, becomes airborne, is then carried on the opposite foot and again becomes airborne."[25] Bare satisfaction of the nonsupport requirement for running produces a version commonly known as jogging. This simple form is characterized by a slow pace, a short stride, and a bouncing motion. Running at increasingly greater velocities leads progressively to the ultimate version, sprinting, which is typified by a fast pace, a long stride, and minimal bounce.

PERFORMANCE TRENDS IN RUNNING

Few investigators have been concerned with the objective measurement of the running speed of preschool children. The performances of children in this age group tend to be erratic, and there is reason to believe that the concept of the sprint effort is quite vague for some of the younger ones. Careful observers have been content to accept the generalization that children progressively increase in speed of running during the preschool age period. At the age of 5, most children have developed reasonably acceptable running form and understand what it means to run fast.

Details of the methods of testing the running speed of school children have varied considerably from one study to another. The diverse procedures have included sprinting for distances ranging from 30 to 50 yards and have provided for standing as well as running starts. Obviously, the results of testing with different procedures are not comparable, but they are informative and give shape to the total picture of running performance. A summary of the studies of motor performances of elementary school children shows a consistent year-to-year improvement in running speed for both boys and girls from age 5 to age 11. Boys tend to have the edge over girls, but at ages 5, 6, and 7 the performances are quite similar. Tabular summaries of studies that produced mean performances in timed dashes by children of elementary school age can be found in Espenschade and in Keogh.[10,20] For a newer reference, Glassow et al. or Milne et al. may be consulted.[16,21]

DEVELOPMENT OF FORM IN RUNNING

Running is a skill that appears at an early age and is a natural part of the development of the modes of locomotion. Prior to the time he can run, the child learns to walk independently and acquires the additional abilities necessary to deal with the demands of the new skill. In particular, the child must have sufficient strength to propel himself upward and forward into the nonsupport phase with one leg. He must also possess the coordination and balance necessary to be able to control the faster movements produced during the running stride. According to Gesell, these abilities or capacities are not present generally before 18 months of age, but by the age of 2 years most children can run well enough to satisfy the minimum standard.[14] However, the transition from one skill to another is not necessarily a smooth one. It has been observed by Burnett and Johnson that although the child might have achieved some of the mature characteristics of walking, he still reverted to an immature pattern when first attempting to run.[4] Characteristic aspects of the reversion were widening of the base, abducting the arms to the high guard position, landing with a flat foot, and having knee extension at midsupport. The investigator's explanation of the phenomenon pointed to Gesell's concept of "reciprocal interweaving" during development in which there is alternation from mature to immature stages.[15] Adjustments are made quickly after the skill is acquired in its most rudimentary form (Fig. 3–1), and there is a continuous process of refinement resulting from the combined influences of maturation and practice. The process may extend well into puberty.[3]

FIG. 3-1. Running form of 18-month-old boy (slow pace).

The child begins by running in a straight line which is the easiest use of the new skill. During play in the preschool years there is an increasing demand for the ability to change direction quickly, to dodge, and to stop abruptly. Gradually the skill of running improves, not only in terms of the speed of body movement, but also in terms of the ability to run in variable patterns and on different surfaces and terrains. Harper studied several variables in the technique 5-year-old boys and girls used to change direction 180 degrees from a full speed run.[18] There was considerable variability in the performances, yet 78% of the reversals were to the left, all were accomplished in 4 to 8 steps, and there was no significant difference between boys and girls in either running velocity or reversal time.

The kinds of problems that arise in connection with the development of throwing, jumping, striking, and other basic skills seem to be missing in the development of running. Unless the child is handicapped, he begins to run without fanfare, and ordinarily the form he displays draws little attention. For many years the systematic study of the development of running was neglected simply because there was no apparent reason to seek additional information. The situation has changed. A growing concern for effective movement during the past decade has stimulated research in the mechanics of most fundamental skills, including running. Recent research has led to an improved understanding of the developmental changes in the patterns of running that parallel the yearly improvements in running speed.

Four important studies represent a significant effort to discover developmental trends in running form. In the first of these, Clouse analyzed the running patterns of 6 carefully selected preschool boys, ages 1½ to 5½ years.[5] For this representative group, running speed increased over the age range and was accompanied by an increase in the length of the stride and a longer nonsupport period. Contributing to these developmental trends were notable changes during various phases of the running stride. With advancing age the support leg was extended more quickly at all joints and was extended more fully at takeoff, the knee of the recovery leg was flexed more, and the thigh of the recovery leg was swung forward faster and higher. Clouse suggested that these characteristics signal improvement in the individual child's running pattern and help identify the more skilled runners.[5] All of these developmental trends can be found in a comparison of the running form of the 18-month-old boy in Figure 3–1 and the much more highly skilled 3-year-old boy in Figure 3–2.

A similar analytic study of running form was done by Dittmer, who used a small group of girls but collected longitudinal data on them.[8] Her subjects were 2 good and 2 poor runners selected at age 6 and studied yearly through age 10. With each successive year there was an increase in speed, in the length of the stride, in the amount of time in the nonsupport phase of the stride, in the velocity of the supporting leg, and in the flexion of the knee of the swinging leg both during recovery and at contact. These trends are consistent with those reported by Clouse. Many of the variables identified as performance trends also were factors differentiating good from poor performers. The good runner in her study was further distinguished by having her total body

FIG. 3–2. Running pattern of a 3-year-old boy who uses effective leg action.

more nearly over her contact foot when it touched the ground and by having her total body farther ahead of her supporting foot immediately prior to takeoff.

Fortney followed the development of the action of the swinging leg in the running patterns of 12 boys over a period of 5 years.[13] Four boys who were above average, 4 who were average, and 4 who were below average in running speed in grade 2 were the subjects in this longitudinal study continued through grade 6. Over the 5-year period there was a tendency to increase the height of the leading thigh at the beginning of the nonsupport phase of the stride. This helped increase the length of the stride and placed the forward leg in a more favorable position for beginning the support phase. A second trend over the period was the progressive amount of flexion of the lower leg, with the heel being brought closer to the buttock on the forward leg swing. These same trends were observed in the younger runners studied by Clouse and in the girls studied by Dittmer. Moreover, Fortney found improvement for all the subjects in her study regardless of their initial classification.[13] However, distinct traits were identified that distinguished the good runners. Good runners brought the thigh of the swinging leg forward faster and through a greater range of movement than the poor runners.

Additionally they had high heel kick-up as the leg was brought forward, and they raised the thigh of the leading leg closer to the horizontal at the end of the forward swing.

The path of the center of gravity during the running stride was the concern of the last of these important studies of developmental form.[2] The running form of 12 boys who had been carefully identified as good runners was studied for 2 consecutive years. Four boys in grades 1, 3, and 5 were studied and then restudied after they had moved on respectively to grades 2, 4, and 6. Beck found that generally the center of gravity of the body moved upward with the propulsion of the support leg and continued upward briefly following takeoff. Then it began to move in a downward path and continued in this direction until after the support foot made contact and began its propulsive effort. The center of gravity of all runners had an undulating, wavelike path. With increased age and speed of running, the wavelike movement became relatively flatter, with the horizontal component increasing more than the vertical component. The boys simply became less bouncy in their running stride as they advanced in age and increased in speed.

The number of subjects in each of the four studies cited was small, but the children were chosen carefully and collectively they represented an extensive age range. Cinematographic analysis of their running form gave evidence of remarkably similar developmental trends that were generally supported by the more extensive Wisconsin study.[16] In summary, the trends were:

1. An increase in the length of the running stride (resulting in an increase in running speed).
2. A decrease in the relative amount of upward movement of the body in each stride.
3. An increase in the extension of the propulsive leg.
4. An increase in the amount of time in the nonsupport phase of the stride.
5. An increase in the closeness of the heel to the buttock on the forward swing of the recovery leg.
6. An increase in the height of the knee at the end of the forward leg swing.
7. A decrease in the relative distance the forward foot is ahead of the center of gravity when it makes contact with the ground.

From these trends it is apparent that the leverage of the limbs involved in running improves with advancing age and contributes to the refinements that result in increased speed of running (Figs. 3–3; 3–4).

FIG. 3–3. A 5-year-old girl with well-coordinated arm and leg action but with typically limited range of movement by arms and legs.

FIG. 3–4. A 7-year-old boy demonstrating extensive arm and leg movement. His arm and leg movements are more advanced than those used by the girl in Figure 3–3. (Drawn from film loaned by Miss Ruth Glassow).

In an effort to make motor pattern identification relatively uncomplicated for teachers, Seefeldt, Reuschlein, and Vogel presented developmental changes in running in the form of stages rather than as trends.[24] The following stages were based upon mixed longitudinal data on approximately 150 children ranging in age from 1½ to 8 years.

STAGE 1. The arms are extended sideward at shoulder height (high-guard position). The stride is short and of shoulder width. The surface contact is made with the entire foot simultaneously. Little knee flexion is seen. The feet remain near the surface at all times.

STAGE 2. Arms are carried at middle guard (waist height), the stride is longer and approaches the midsagittal line. The surface contact is usually with the entire foot, striking simultaneously. Greater knee flexion is noted in the restraining phase. The swing leg is flexed and the movement of the legs becomes anteroposterior.

STAGE 3. The arms are no longer used primarily for balance. Arms are carried below waist level and may flex and assume a counter rotary action. The foot contact is heel–toe. Stride length increases, and both feet move along a midsagittal line. The swing leg flexion may be as great as 90 degrees.

STAGE 4. Foot contact is heel–toe at slow or modest velocities but may be entirely on the metatarsal arch while sprinting. Arm action is in direct opposition to leg action. Knee flexion is used to maintain the momentum during the support phase. The swing leg may flex until it is nearly in contact with the buttocks during its recovery phase.

The stages obviously do not include all of the trends outlined earlier in this section, but rather, they highlight some movement characteristics which represent changes to more advanced levels of skill.

Up to this point, developmental running form has been studied almost exclusively from the side view and analysis has been limited mostly to the movements of the legs. Important rotatory movements occurring around the vertical axis of the body can be observed effectively only when the perspective is changed by moving the vantage point 90 degrees for a frontal or dorsal view of the runner. From this angle, twisting and turning movements involving the arms, trunk, and legs appear to be natural and essential to the movement pattern of running. Unfortunately the literature on motor pattern development is virtually devoid of studies concerning the precise nature of these rotatory movements and their influence on developmental form. The observations that follow, therefore, must be considered tentative and open to modification following further study.

During the earliest stages of running, the movement pattern seems to be characterized by extensive movements around the long axis of the body. The extent to which some of the exaggerated movements can be observed is dependent upon the willingness of the child to run with full effort. The 24-month-old boy in Figure 3–5 was running with unusual abandon and had difficulty maintaining balance at the rapid pace. Some aspects of his leg action illustrate movements that appear commonly in the running patterns of young children and with progressively less frequency in the patterns of older children. The movements of the recovery leg are of particular interest when viewed from the back. The knee of the recovery leg swings outward and then around and forward in preparation for the support phase. In young children, this knee action is accompanied by a toeing-out of the foot of the recovery leg. Aside from the natural tendency for the child to abduct his foot, the toeing-out appears to be a possible adjustment that allows the foot to be swung forward without being raised more than a few inches. Later, when the outward rotatory movement of the knee is more vigorous, it produces a sequence in which the foot first crosses the midline of the body before moving around and forward (Fig. 3–6). These exaggerated leg and foot movements are lessened progressively

FIG. 3–5. Posterior view of a 24-month-old boy running with unusual effort. His speed produces precarious balance which he counters by arm movements in the horizontal plane. The outward swing of the knee of his recovery leg is also apparent.

FIG. 3–6. Exaggerated rotation during the beginning of the swing phase causes the foot of the recovery leg to cross the midline before passing under the trunk.

in the development toward mature running form. A regular increase in the length of the running stride contributes significantly to the elimination of some of the less productive rotatory leg movements.

Perhaps one trend concerning the rotatory action of the legs in the running pattern can be added tentatively to the developmental trends observed from the side view. The additional trend is progressively less outward swing of the knee of the recovery leg and correspondingly less toe-out by the foot during the swinging phase.

Arm movements in the running pattern have been classified predominantly as automatic reactions. For every action by the legs in a developmental running pattern there seems to be an accompanying and predictable reaction by the arms. For example, in the earliest stage of running when pace is slow and the legs are relatively straight (Fig. 3–1), there is little bend in the arms. During the same period when the stride is short, the arc through which the arms swing is also short. When the knee of the recovery leg swings out to the side and then forward, the opposite arm makes an exaggerated hooking motion forward toward the midline of the body. If the support leg is straight and thrusting vigorously, the opposite arm remains relatively straight and swings obliquely outward to balance the heavier lever and to balance the outwardly swinging knee. The persistence of these basic adjustive arm actions at different ages is emphasized in Figure 3–7. The arm moves outward and backward while remaining nearly straight and loops inward at the back end of the arc. On the forward swing, the arm moves closer

FIG. 3-7. Children of various ages demonstrating similar arm patterns. From left, 1½-year-old, 2-year-old, 2-year-old, 5-year-old, 4-year-old, 3-year-old, and 6-year-old. The arm on the forward swing crosses the midline of the body, and the opposite arm swings outward and then loops inward at the end of the backswing.

to the trunk, is bent more at the elbow, and swings quickly toward the midline of the body. Minor differences in the amount of arm movement by children at the various ages can be observed, but the similarities are apparent. They suggest several trends in the developmental form of arm action in running.

1. The hand hooks less toward the midline of the trunk at the end of the forward swing, and the arm loops outward less on the backswing.
2. The arms swing through a longer arc in the anteroposterior plane.
3. The arms are bent more toward a right angle at the elbow.

These trends represent development toward what is regarded generally as a mature pattern of arm action in running. They do not include the high guard and middle guard arm positions in which the arms are used to help maintain balance.

MATURE PATTERN OF RUNNING

The discussion of developmental running patterns was based upon the performance of the child when he was attempting to run at maximum velocity. The approach was consistent with the use of the sprint pace as a basis for determining mature running form. An impelling reason for using the sprint is the relatively constant type of performance it yields.[7] The high degree of effort required produces maximum movement and a reasonably stable pattern.

FIG. 3–8. Mature form in running at the sprint pace.

In a complete cycle of the running pattern each leg goes through a support phase and a recovery phase, and the full sequence produces two periods of nonsupport (Fig. 3–8). The essentials of the mature pattern can be summarized as follows:

1. The trunk maintains a slight forward lean throughout the stride pattern.
2. Both arms swing through a large arc in an oblique vertical plane and in synchronized opposition to the leg action.
3. Complete extension of the support leg at the hip, knee, and ankle propels the body forward and upward into the nonsupport phase.
4. As the recovery leg swings forward quickly to a high knee raise, the lower part of the leg flexes, bringing the heel close to the buttock.
5. The backward moving foot of the recovery leg contacts the ground approximately flat and under the center of gravity.
6. The knee of the support leg bends slightly after the foot has made contact with the ground.

The pattern outlined is fundamentally in agreement with the findings of Fenn,[11] Altfillisch,[1] Finley,[12] Deshon and Nelson,[6] Slocum and James,[25] James and Brubaker,[19] Dillman,[7] and others who have studied various aspects of sprinting form. The evidence they have provided is particularly applicable in the more detailed examination of the various parts of the basic pattern in the following sections.

The Forward Trunk Lean

The forward trunk lean is slightly greater in sprinting than in running at any lesser pace, but the trunk should still be nearly erect. The sprinter must adjust for the additional amount of air resistance he encounters (it varies roughly with the square of his velocity), and he must position his pelvis during propulsion to allow for the full, effective extension of his leg. Altfillisch reported a forward lean of 20 to 25 degrees from the vertical but did not indicate the means for measuring the angle.[1] Some of the confusion regarding this aspect of form can be blamed on a misunderstanding of the difference between forward trunk lean and total body lean. Dyson suggested that there is an illusion of exaggerated forward lean in sprinting due to the extreme body position at the moment the propulsive leg is thrusting the body into flight (Fig. 3–8).[9] The angle of the total body, including the propulsive leg, measured at the push-off is quite different from the angle of forward lean of just the trunk. James and Brubaker explain that "Excessive forward lean reduces mobility of the lumbar spine-pelvic unit, reduces hip flexion relative to the running surface, prevents maximum forward placement of the recovery foot, places excessive stress on the foot at foot strike, and requires additional effort from the postural muscles to maintain balance."[19]

The Arm Action

Arm action in running is compensatory and synchronous with the action of the legs. Since the leg action in sprinting is forceful and extensive, the arms must move in like manner. The hand swings nearly to shoulder level and slightly toward the midline of the body on the forward swing, and the elbow reaches almost as high on the back swing, bringing the hand back beyond the hip. Both shoulders might be raised slightly at the ends of the swing because of the forceful and extreme arm movement, but this elevation should be achieved without producing tension.

During the excursion of the arms in the forward-backward movement, the angle of the elbow changes somewhat in many expert sprinters. The angle increases on the downward movement of the backward swing and decreases to about a right angle on the upward swing of the backward movement. This position is retained on the forward swing until just before the end when the angle tends to decrease slightly. Altfillisch found there was a difference of approximately 6 inches in the height of the path of the hand during forward and backward swings.[1] According to his findings, the path of the wrist was below the hip line on the backward swing and above it on the forward swing. It is reasonable to expect the arm to straighten a bit on the downward part of the backswing because the leg with which it is in opposition has its greatest vertical leverage during that phase of the stride, and the slightly extended arm is a better compensating lever.

Contact by the Support Foot

The support foot contacts the ground approximately under the body's center of gravity. If contact is ahead of or behind this point during the full sprint stride, the effectiveness of leg propulsion is diminished. Contact ahead of the optimum point produces a braking effect, and contact behind it reduces the range of propulsive effort. If the runner's foot contacts the ground at an effective point relative to his center of gravity, his foot is virtually flat when it lands. Practically all of the 33 sprinters studied by Fenn came down flat-footed or slightly on the heel when running at full speed.[11] A few runners touched down on the side of the foot, presumably because of the tendency for the foot to supinate in the nonsupport position. Analysis of film showing Olympic-class sprinters revealed that the ball of the foot touches fractionally before the rest of the sole and confirmed that the heel subsequently contacts the ground.[22] It is important that sprinters not be taught to "run on their toes" because the wrong foot position at contact can interfere with the mechanics of effective leg action.

Action of the Support Leg

Immediately after the foot contacts the ground, the knee of the support leg bends slightly to stop the downward movement of the center of gravity and to allow the body weight to move forward smoothly with a minimum of wasteful upward and downward movement.[11] Bending at the knee after the foot has been planted has the additional effect of creating a favorable change at the ankle joint. The amount of dorsiflexion at the ankle is increased as much as 12 degrees before the beginning of extension, thereby increasing the effective distance over which the foot can thrust.

The actual propulsive force of the support leg is a backward, downward thrust produced by extension at the hip, the knee, and the ankle. This force raises the center of gravity slightly and pushes the body upward and forward into the nonsupport phase.

The propulsive effort of the support leg in sprinting produces maximum effective forward force. The emphasis on the forward component of force results in a long stride and a minimal amount of body rise. After examining the amount of body rise of 18 college athletes running at various velocities, Rapp concluded that body rise and running speed are inversely related; i.e., body rise was significantly greater at a long distance pace than at a sprint pace.[23] In the smooth running style of the expert sprinter, it is difficult to observe any body rise even though there is a minor vertical excursion of his center of gravity during each stride.

Action of the Leg During Recovery

Immediately after takeoff into the nonsupport phase, the support leg begins the important recovery or swinging phase. The knee begins to swing forward quickly as the lower leg flexes, bringing the heel of the foot of the recovery leg close to the buttock (Fig. 3–8). In effect, this bending action reduces the resistance leverage against the swinging leg, permitting it to move forward quickly, and at the same time "the vigorous forward swing of the recovery extremity increases ground reaction of the support extremity and enhances forward thrust."[19]

The thigh of the recovery leg reaches the height of its forward swing at approximately the same time the toe of the support leg leaves the ground. At that instant, the thigh of the swing leg begins to rotate backward, and the lower leg begins to extend. Just before the foot of the recovery leg contacts the ground, it is moving backward at a rate roughly equal to the forward speed of the body.[25]

SELECTED MECHANICAL PRINCIPLES APPLICABLE TO RUNNING

Running is one of the few basic skills in which the pattern of movements is performed repeatedly without interruption. Several mechanical principles are related to the process of maintaining effective continuity of motion in the running pattern. Three of the principles that are directly applicable are:

1. For every action there is a reaction that is equal in amount and opposite in direction (arm–leg opposition helps deal with reaction).
2. A short lever has less reaction than a long lever when moved through the same range at the same speed (bending the knee of the recovery leg shortens the lever and makes it easier to bring forward).
3. Force must be applied to change the velocity of a body (each

nonsupport phase causes a slight loss of velocity and force must be applied by the support leg to maintain continuity of motion).

ADAPTATIONS OF THE BASIC PATTERN OF RUNNING

Common adaptations of the basic pattern result from progressively decreasing the pace from the sprint through the paces for the middle distance and distance down to the jog. The sprint is the fastest pace in running and is at the same time the most vigorous form. It requires a high degree of energy expenditure and therefore cannot be continued except for short distances. A sprinter, when running a 100-meter dash, accelerates for approximately the first 40 meters before he attains his maximal running velocity.[7] That peak velocity in running, however, can be maintained only for a relatively short distance. The mature sprinter soon experiences the unavoidable but barely perceptible decline in his running velocity even though he continues to run with full effort. Because the energy cost of running at the sprint pace is exorbitant, adjustments in pace must be made when the runner seeks an effective performance at longer than sprint distances. Concomitant to decreases in running pace are changes in form or movement pattern. The significant changes in form that accompany a *progressive reduction in pace* are included in the following outline.

1. Action of arms
   a. Arms move through a shorter arc.
   b. Arms bend slightly more at the elbows.
   c. Arms swing more across the trunk toward the midline.
   d. Shoulders are elevated less at both ends of the arm swing.
2. Action of recovery leg
   a. Knee raise at the forward end of the leg swing is less.
   b. Knee flexion and heel raise on the swing-through are less.
3. Action of propulsive leg
   a. Foot lands farther forward in relation to the center of gravity.
   b. Propulsive leg extends less at takeoff.
   c. Propulsive leg movement is slower and the time in the support phase is increased.
4. Amount of body rise increases.
5. Amount of forward trunk lean decreases.

Collectively these changes produce a shorter stride, a slower pace, and a more economical pattern of running. Some of the differences in form are minor but appear in the running patterns illustrated in Figure 3–9. If the changes in movement pattern produced by a reduction in pace are present when the child or adult runs as fast as he can, the form is actually less than mature. The importance of maximum speed must therefore be emphasized when running form is being evaluated.

880

mile

2 mile

FIG. 3–9. College track men running at different paces during competition. Upper, 880 yard pace; middle, 1 mile pace; lower, 2 mile pace.

ANALYSIS OF FORM IN RUNNING

Key aspects of the movement pattern used in running can be observed quite easily because the pattern is repeated and the observer has successive opportunities to appraise each feature. When analyzing a runner's form, the following specific questions might be asked:

1. Does he extend his leg fully at takeoff?
2. Does his heel come close to his buttock during recovery?
3. Does his knee rise well at the end of recovery?
4. Does his foot land relatively flat and under his body?
5. Is his trunk slightly forward with his head in proper alignment?
6. Do his arms swing slightly toward his midline with elbows bent?
7. Has he eliminated exaggerated rotary movement around his long axis?

The answers to these questions disclose immature aspects of form but do not quantify the extent of the deviations. It should be remembered that the same relative degree of maturity will be seen in several movements because of the interrelatedness of the movements in the pattern and that arm action is the most variable feature in immature form.

FIG. 3–10. Running form of a 9-year-old girl.

FIG. 3–11. Running form of a 9-year-old boy.

FIG. 3–12. Running form of a 4-year-old boy.

Practice in the analysis of form in running should begin with the developmental sequences in this chapter. Figures 3-1, 3-2, 3-3, 3-4, 3-10, 3-11, and 3-12 can be analyzed for relative pattern maturity as determined by the seven questions proposed. The figures can also be checked for compliance with the characteristics in each of the four stages recommended by Seefeldt, Reuschlein, and Vogel.[24] After the preliminary work with analysis has been completed, there should be an attempt to observe the developmental features in live sprinters (preferably children).

BIBLIOGRAPHY

1. Altfillisch, J.: A Mechanical Analysis of Starting and Running. Unpublished Master's Thesis. University of Iowa, 1947.
2. Beck, M.: The Path of the Center of Gravity During Running in Boys Grades One to Six. Unpublished Doctoral Dissertation, University of Wisconsin, 1966.
3. Bernstein, N. A.: The Coordination and Regulation of Movements. Oxford, Pergamon Press, 1967.
4. Burnett, C. N., and Johnson, E. W.: Development of gait in childhood: Part II. Dev. Med. Child Neurol., *13*:207, 1971.
5. Clouse, F.: A Kinematic Analysis of the Development of the Running Pattern of Preschool Boys. Unpublished Doctoral Dissertation, University of Wisconsin, 1959.
6. Deshon, D. E., and Nelson, R. C.: A cinematographical analysis of sprint running. Res. Q. Am. Assoc. Health Phys. Educ., *35*:451, 1964.
7. Dillman, C.: Kinematic analyses of running. *In* Exercise and Sport Sciences Reviews, Vol. III (Wilmore and Keogh, eds.). New York, Academic Press, 1975.
8. Dittmer, J.: A Kinematic Analysis of the Development of the Running Pattern of Grade School Girls and Certain Factors Which Distinguish Good From Poor Performance at the Observed Ages. Unpublished Master's Thesis, University of Wisconsin, 1962.
9. Dyson, G.: The Mechanics of Athletics. London, University of London Press, 1970.
10. Espenschade, A.: Motor development. *In* Science and Medicine of Exercise and Sports (Johnson, ed.). New York, Harper and Brothers, 1960.
11. Fenn, W. O.: Work against gravity and work due to velocity changes in running. Am. J. Physiol., *93*:433, 1930.
12. Finley, R.: Kinesiological Analysis of Human Motion. Unpublished Doctoral Thesis, Springfield College, 1961.
13. Fortney, V.: The Swinging Limb in Running of Boys Ages Seven Through Eleven. Unpublished Master's Thesis, University of Wisconsin, 1964.
14. Gesell, A.: The First Five Years of Life. New York, Harper and Brothers, 1940.
15. Gesell, A.: The ontogenesis of infant behavior. *In* Manual of Child Psychology (Carmichael, ed.). New York, Wiley, 1954.
16. Glassow, R. B., Halverson, L. E., and Rarick, G. L.: Improvement of Motor Development and Physical Fitness in Elementary School Children. Cooperative Research Project No. 696, University of Wisconsin, 1965.
17. Gundlach, H.: "Research on the relationship between the kind of stride and speed of masculine and feminine sprinters of different qualifications," Wiss. Z. DHFK (Leipzig), *2*: 1959/60.
18. Harper, C.: Movement Responses of Kindergarten Children to a Change of Direction Task—An Analysis of Selected Measures. Unpublished Master's Thesis, University of Wisconsin, 1975.
19. James, S., and Brubaker, C. E.: Biomechanical and neuromuscular aspects of running. *In* Exercise and Sport Sciences Reviews, Vol. I (Wilmore, ed.). New York, Academic Press, 1973.

20. Keogh, J.: Motor Performance of Elementary School Children. Department of Physical Education, University of California, Los Angeles, 1965.
21. Milne, C., Seefeldt, V., and Haubenstricker, J.: Longitudinal Trends in Motor Performance in Children. Abstracts of Research Papers, AAHPER, Washington, D. C., 1971.
22. Nett, T.: Foot Plant in Running. Track Technique No. 15, March 1964, pp. 462–463.
23. Rapp, K.: Running Velocity: Body-Rise and Stride Length. Unpublished Master's Thesis, University of Iowa, 1963.
24. Seefeldt, V., Reuschlein, S., and Vogel, P.: Sequencing Motor Skills Within the Physical Education Curriculum. Paper presented at the AAHPER meeting, Houston, 1972.
25. Slocum, D. B., and James, S. L.: Biomechanics of running. J.A.M.A., *205*:11, 97, 1968.

4

JUMPING

Simple as well as specialized forms of hopping, leaping, and hurdling are clustered in a general category of skills called jumps. A jump is accomplished by propelling the body off the ground with the thrust from one or both legs. The method of launching the body into the air is the essential ingredient of the jump, but in many instances the method of landing is important to minimal form or to skillful performance. Consequently, most descriptions of jumping skills specify that contact be reestablished by landing on one or both feet and that balance be retained after landing.

JUMPING ACHIEVEMENTS OF PRESCHOOL CHILDREN

By the time a child has developed the ability to run he has also acquired the physical abilities necessary to jump. When he propels himself forward and upward into flight with one foot and lands on the other while running, technically he has satisfied the minimal requirement for a successful jump. Jumping, however, ordinarily is associated with more vigorous and extensive nonsupport movements and should be regarded as a more difficult skill. A child needs more than just enough strength to thrust his body into the air if he is to be prepared adequately for a successful assault on the awaiting array of jumping skills. He must also be capable of coordinating more elaborate movements while maintaining balance, or he will be ineffective in accommodating the complexities of the new skills. In addition to the physical prerequisites, there are the nebulous qualities of courage and confidence that are of major importance. Gutteridge and others have observed that children are apt to revert to an earlier mode of jumping when the height of the jump is increased or when a new type of jump is introduced.[11] The child's

FIG. 4–1. Upper: 37-month-old boy showing a vigorous jump down from a two-footed takeoff to a two-footed landing. Note the compensatory "winging" of the arms and the slight unevenness of the feet. Lower: 33-month-old girl using the step-down form that leads toward her first downward jump.

speculation regarding the difficulty of each new jump is one of the critical factors influencing the rate at which he acquires jumping skill.

A child foregoes his independence and opts for the security of a helping hand when performing the step-down that usually precedes his first effort at jumping. He grasps someone's hand for balance and from a support on one foot steps down, contacting a lower level with his opposite foot (Fig. 4–1). The child is just degrees away from performing his first true jump after he is able to walk down a step holding the hand of an adult. By an increase in the length of the step, a quick lift-off by the support foot, a brief nonsupport period followed by a balanced landing on the foot of the forward leg, a real jump has been achieved. The jump is done rather rigidly at first with the support and lead legs remaining relatively straight and with the arms in opposition but elevated sideward for balance. As the step-down jump is done less gingerly and more confidently, the outward lunge caused by a straight support leg is reduced and the step is shortened. Changes in form accompanying the shortened step are a quicker and higher lift of the support leg to enhance the flight phase and a greater lift from the arms with a slight retraction of the shoulders for balance.

The child moves from the step-down jump through a general sequence of achievements marked by increased heights and new types of jumps. It is during the third and fourth years of his life that he makes rapid progress in the development of jumping skill

TABLE 4–1. JUMPING ACHIEVEMENTS OF PRESCHOOL CHILDREN

Achievement	Motor Age (months)	Source
Jump from 12 inch height; one foot	24	M&W
Jump off floor; both feet	28	B
Jump from 18 inch height; one foot	31	M&W
Jump from chair 26 cm. high; both feet	32	B
Jump from 8 inch height; both feet	33	M&W
Jump from 12 inch height; both feet	34	M&W
Jump from 18 inch height; both feet	37	M&W
Jump from 30 cm. height; both feet	37.1	B
Jump forward 10–35 cm. from 30 cm. height; both feet	37.3	B
Hop on two feet 1–3 times	38	M&W
Jump over rope 20 cm. high; both feet	41.5	B
Hop on one foot 1–3 times	43	B

Adapted from information in studies by Bayley and McCaskill and Wellman.[2,25]

TABLE 4–2. TYPES OF JUMPS ACHIEVED BY CHILDREN
IN TERMS OF PROGRESSIVE DIFFICULTY

Jump down from one foot to the other foot.
Jump up from two feet to two feet.
Jump down from one foot to two feet.
Jump down from two feet to two feet.
Run and jump forward from one foot to the other.
Jump forward from two feet to two feet.
Run and jump forward from one foot to two feet.
Jump over object from two feet to two feet.
Jump from one foot to same foot rhythmically.

---

as measured by specific achievements. Bayley and McCaskill and Wellman have chronicled some of the skills demonstrated by children of preschool age and have tentatively assigned a motor age to each (Table 4–1).[2,25] The range in motor performances of children is so wide that the task of assigning a precise age expectation to a particular achievement is a risky business. Thus there is wisdom in giving a tentative label to the age assignments for the achievement of jumping skills.

Another and perhaps more useful way to view the jumping achievements of young children is in terms of jumping technique or type of jump. This approach is more concerned with whether the child can jump down from one foot before he can do it from two feet than it is with whether he can jump down with one foot from a height of 18 inches before he can jump down with two feet from a height of 12 inches. This approach is speculative to some extent because there are voids in the data needed to support a particular progression of types of jumps. Because many of the jumping skills have been studied in isolation rather than in relation to one another, the relative difficulty of each must be based partly upon suggestive rather than fully substantive data. A list of types of jumps arranged tentatively in order of development appears in Table 4–2. The time interval between the achievement of the different types of jumps is quite variable. It ranges from a considerable time lag to almost simultaneous achievement. After the child can perform a particular type of jump, he normally improves in his performance of the jump by increasing height or distance.

PERFORMANCE TRENDS IN JUMPING SKILL

Data published by Bayley, Gutteridge and McCaskill and Wellman stand as evidence of regular progress in the development of jumping skill by preschool children.[2,11,25] The children who were subjects in these studies were tested on a wide variety of discrete jumping tasks. Their performances showed that they were able to do jumping tasks of greater difficulty at each successive preschool year. The jumping performance of the school-age child is more frequently measured by the vertical jump or by the standing broad jump than it is by a series of diverse tasks. Performances by children in the jump and reach test are better each year, starting at the age of 5 years, according to Jenkins and Wilson.[19,33] They verified the trend of yearly improvement and also found a superiority of boys over girls in this type of jump. The standing long jump currently is a more popular standard measure of the comparative jumping ability of school children than the vertical jump. Keogh summarized the results of eleven studies done over a 35-year period that contained data on the performances of school children in the standing long jump.[21] He found variations in the mean performances reported, but concluded that there was a consistent linear improvement at successive ages and grade levels. There were no important differences in performance between boys and girls in the standing long jump until age 8, when boys were the better performers. At ages 9 and 10 the boys were about 1 year or 3 to 5 inches in distance ahead of the girls. Contrary results on the sex differences in standing long jump performance were reported in a study in which the school children had participated in a special program that was designed to improve strength, develop skill, and stimulate organic function. Girls did not fall behind when given the benefit of a physically stimulating physical activity program. Standing long jump performances for boys and girls were essentially the same at ages 7 through 12 years.[10]

DEVELOPMENTAL FORM IN THE VERTICAL JUMP

The child can perform a minimal vertical jump at an early age, but his technique at times is wildly variable and unpredictable. When his movements finally congeal into a detectable pattern, it is identified by (1) minimal preliminary crouch, (2) sideward elevation of arms and shoulders, (3) small forward lean at takeoff, and (4) quick flexion at hips and knees following takeoff. Halverson et al. discovered two of these features when studying the development of hopping with very young children.[14] Arms were raised to middle or high guard position and instead of providing an upward thrust, the hopping leg was quickly raised to cause the body to become airborne.

Some aspects of form are dependent upon whether the jump involves reaching for an object or is simply general upward movement. In an informal film study, a small group of 4-year-old children were asked to jump as high as they could. The responses were highly individualistic, but there were two common elements in the form displayed: the shoulders were hunched upward followed by outbalancing motions with the arms, and the legs were drawn up well under the body immediately after lift-off (Fig. 4–4). An interesting transition in form occurred when the set task was changed, and the children were asked to jump up and try to touch the tester's hand. The arms were lifted well and the whole body was thrust into full extension (Fig. 4–2). Poe verified the importance of using an overhead target to elicit an effective vertical jump from young children.[27] Sixteen of 22 children between the ages of 23 and 35 months were able to complete the task of jumping vertically to touch a target. These successes suggest that Hellebrandt's observation that a young child cannot propel his body into the air by simultaneous

FIG. 4–2. Position of 4-year-old children at the height of a vertical jump in which they reached for an object. Their bodies are fully extended with a slight forward lean. The two boys use effective arm opposition.

extension of both legs is based more upon the complexity of the attempted task than upon the child's actual capability.[17]

The movement characteristics of a group of 2-year-old children as they performed a vertical jump were described by Poe.[27] She dealt with both the overt configurations and the kinematics of the performances and then compared the findings to a model provided by a skilled adult performer. Six patterns were identified, but they could not be ranked confidently because three contained adultlike as well as immature traits. Despite this problem, the range of displacement at ankles, knees, hips, and arms increased steadily from Pattern I to Pattern VI, suggesting trendlike motor pattern improvement. One-third of the 2-year-old children employed the most adultlike pattern (VI) which included a moderate to deep preparatory crouch, forceful upward flexion of both arms in conjunction with lower extremity extension, and nearly complete body extension in flight. Pattern V was slightly closer to the adult pattern when patterns were compared on the basis of key aspects of body configuration, but Pattern VI more closely paralleled the adult pattern in a comparison of displacement and velocity measurements.

Wilson studied the changes in form in the jump and reach version of the vertical jump at successive ages from 4 to 11 years.[33] Improvement in form for this age group was noted in terms of:

1. A small progressive increase in crouch.
2. More effective arm lift.
3. Improved extension at takeoff and in flight.
4. Greater extension of the trunk at the crest of the reach.

Similar results came to light from longitudinal data on two girls who were studied over a 2-year period starting at age 3 years.[28] The subjects showed increased flexion at the knees during the preparatory crouch, increased extension throughout the body at takeoff, and more effective arm action during the upward thrust.

Effective form during an early stage of the developmental period is demonstrated by the 4-year-old boy in Figure 4–3 as he jumps and reaches. His crouch causes his legs to be bent at the knee slightly in excess of 90 degrees. Upward movement is initiated with both arms followed immediately by extension at the hips, knees, and ankles. His body is fully extended after the takeoff and at the crest of the jump. The side view shows the typical tendency to jump forward slightly at the takeoff. One aspect of his form that is not particularly effective is the action of his nonreaching arm in the upper series of the illustration. In the lower sequence showing a back view, his form improves when his nonreaching arm is swung downward in reaction as the other arm stretches upward. Similar body extension, forward jump, and arm opposition can be observed in the children in Figure 4–2. If the vertical jump does not require purposeful reaching by the

FIG. 4–3. Lateral and posterior views of a 4-year-old boy doing a vertical jump. Upper: He crouches, lifts his arms, and thrusts his body upward and slightly forward into full extension. Lower: More effective arm opposition but also more forward reach.

FIG. 4–4. Immature form in the vertical jump. "Winging" arm action, incomplete extension, quick flexion of the legs, and slight forward jump.

arms, less mature arm and leg action is seen in the jumping pattern (Fig. 4–4). When the arms have a particular task, the head extends as the eyes focus upon the objective of the impending arm action. This head position is conducive to effective body extension during the jump. By contrast, the head flexion in Figure 4–4 is consistent with the ineffective tuck or flexion that pervades the entire jumping pattern.

MATURE PATTERN IN THE VERTICAL JUMP

The sequence of movements in the mature pattern of the vertical jump is comparatively uncomplicated. When the special arm actions that occur after the takeoff are disregarded temporarily, the fundamental pattern consists of four movements in the following sequence:

1. There is flexion at hips, knees, and ankles during the preparatory crouch.
2. The jump begins with a vigorous forward and upward lift by the arms.
3. The thrust is continued by forceful extension at the hips, knees, and ankles.
4. The body remains in extension until the feet are ready to retouch, and then the ankles, knees, and hips flex to absorb the shock of landing.

The concept of an effective basic pattern in the vertical jump was verified in a study by Haldeman.[12] He selected the 5 best vertical jumpers from 806 junior and senior high school boys and studied the techniques they used in jumping. His analysis showed a similar pattern of movements for all 5 jumpers. Although they used a common pattern of movements, the jumpers varied in such details as the amount of flexion at the hip and the trunk in the preparatory crouch and the movement of the nonreaching arm.

Some of the details of the basic pattern have been isolated for study. The effect of foot spacing on the performance in the vertical jump was the detail studied by Willson.[32] He tested a group of 160 male subjects between the ages of 13 and 15 on sixteen different foot spacings. According to his findings, the vertical jump scores decreased progressively as the anteroposterior foot spacing increased, and scores also decreased when lateral spacing exceeded 10 inches. Martin and Stull used college age males as subjects and also determined that lateral foot spacing between 5 and 10 inches was better than 0 or 15-inch spacing.[24] However, their results on anteroposterior foot spacing disagreed with those of Willson.[32] Vertical jump performance was better in their study when anteroposterior spread was 5 to 10 inches with a slight preference for the closer spacing.

The effectiveness of various angles of the knee at the end of the preparatory crouch was studied by Heess.[16] He used 108 eighth grade boys as subjects, and each performed vertical jumps with preliminary knee angles of 45, 65, 90, 115, and 135 degrees. The angles of 65 and 90 degrees produced the best jumps, and the extreme angle of 135 degrees produced the poorest. The college men tested by Martin and Stull, by contrast, performed best with a knee angle of 115 degrees and better at 90 than at 65 degrees.[24] The authors suggest practice or learning effect might be the cause for the different results. It seems clear that an effective crouch is possible for individuals within a rather wide range, but the shallow and deep positions should be avoided.

Arm Action in the Vertical Jump

The girls studied by Lewis demonstrated that arms have a favorable influence on performance in the vertical jump.[23] They jumped higher when their arms were used than when their arms were restricted. An explanation for the improved performance was provided in a study of the use of the force platform in athletics activities. Proper arm action raised the center of gravity to the highest possible point prior to takeoff, and the

FIG. 4–5. Mature form in the vertical jump and reach. There is a preparatory crouch. Then the arms begin the upward movement, followed quickly by extension at the hips, knees, and ankles. As one arm reaches upward, the other swings downward sharply in opposition.

vigorous upward arm swing evoked extra force for the propulsion of the body.[26]

The movement pattern of the arms depends upon the purpose of the jump. When there is no special task for the arms, arm action could be mostly a shoulder shrug with the arms not rising above shoulder level during the jump. If the task is to grasp a rebounding basketball or to grasp a horizontal bar, both arms move directly upward at the same time and reach for their common goal. In the jump ball in basketball and in the jump and reach test, the nonreaching arm is pushed downward just prior to the peak of the jump. That final downward arm movement tilts the shoulder girdle laterally and raises the hand of the reaching arm higher in reaction (Fig. 4–5).

Leg Action in the Vertical Jump

Following the initial movement by the arms, powerful forces from the hips and the legs are applied to thrust the body upward. In close and overlapping succession, there is extension at the hips, the knees, and the ankles with the forces which provide the movement at the hips and the knees being the most powerful.[1]

The sequence of movements in the mature pattern remains constant, but the range of motion at the involved joints varies from one individual to another. The optimal crouch for the vertical jump is an individual matter but includes an effective angle at the hip as well as at the knee. Couper found good jumpers had more erect trunks at the low point of the prejump crouch than poor jumpers.[7] The athlete in Figure 4–5 demonstrates well how the trunk remains in a relatively upright position during the crouch and the jump. He also shows the mature pattern of hip, knee, and ankle extension in the leg thrust.

DEVELOPMENTAL FORM IN THE STANDING LONG JUMP

The vertical jump represents one of the two major directions in which jumps are oriented, and the standing long jump represents the other. There are many elements of a common pattern in the two forms of jumps despite the basic difference in the intended direction of each.

The vertical jump and the standing long jump seem to rise from a common origin. Both first appear as a vertical jump from two feet with a slightly forward takeoff angle. Hellebrandt et al. recognized the basic similarity when they reported that the early form in the standing long jump is more like a bipedal hop than a forward jump for distance.[17] From the common forward-upward direction at the beginning, the vector of one jump moves increasingly toward the vertical and the vector of the other toward the horizontal. As the direction of the thrust in the standing long jump progresses from the vertical toward the horizontal, there are accompanying changes in overt form. Among these changes that indicate progress toward the mature pattern are:

1. An increase in the preliminary crouch.
2. An increase in the forward swing of the arms in the anteroposterior plane.
3. A decrease in the takeoff angle.
4. More complete body extension at takeoff.
5. An increase in thigh flexion during flight.
6. A decrease in the angle of the leg at the instant of landing.

These trends express the changes in movement pattern that contribute to improved effectiveness in the standing long jump. Most of the changes begin to occur fairly promptly, but progress variably, and are complicated by the problem of precarious balance as well as the tendency to use a one-footed takeoff (Fig.

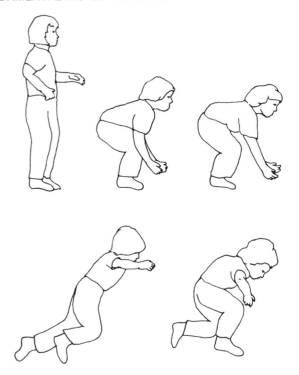

FIG. 4–6. Form used in the standing long jump by a 5-year-old girl. It is a unitary pattern with semistepping leg action. Her arms move sideward for balance and downward and backward to compensate for in-flight forward leg action. (Drawn from film loaned by Miss Ruth Glassow.)

4–6). The coordination of arm and leg movements required merely to launch the body forward into the air from two feet is awkward and unnatural for the child, and coordination is even more difficult if he tries to jump vigorously. Thus it is quite common to see a one-footed takeoff or landing, a "winging" arm movement, or high-guard arm position in the pattern of an immature jumper.

Synchronization of the action of both legs at takeoff, in flight, and at landing is difficult because it is a significant departure from the natural stepping action the child acquires when learning to walk and run. Children often revert to stepping at various times during the developmental period but gradually become able to synchronize the action of both legs in all phases of the jump.

The earliest pattern of arm movement in long jumping from a two-footed takeoff is the counterproductive "winging" motion.

As the body is thrust forward and upward into flight, the shoulders are retracted and the arms are swung backward and upward in the opposite direction. Fortunately, extreme "winging" does not persist but gives way to a sideward lift to a high-guard arm position. The high-guard position with arms raised sideward to more or less shoulder level helps immensely in the maintenance of balance, but has little other value. This equilibratory arm action in the frontal plane typically appears as a part of a unitary pattern in which most movements in the jump occur simultaneously. Little by little the arms move forward with an anteroposterior swing and begin to contribute directly to the development of propulsive force (Fig. 4–7). Spontaneous dorsiflexion and ventroflection of the head occurs during the long jump to keep the head in the proper position in relation to gravity. The precise adjustments are related to the levels of effort and skill development and are thought to be important in the facilitation of performance in vigorous jumping.[17,31]

FIG. 4–7. Form used in the standing long jump by a 4-year-old boy. His preliminary arm swing moves his body forward, but his forward arm action is not well-coordinated with his leg and hip extension. His arm action is slow and incomplete, but it is performed mostly in the proper plane.

Some of the features of the jump that change during the developmental period have been shown to differentiate quality of performance within a group. Halverson found that the inclination of the leg at takeoff and at landing distinguished the good jumpers among a group of kindergarten children.[13] The good performers had a more horizontal takeoff angle, and they had a more horizontal thigh position at landing. Range and speed of movement at the hip and the knee joints were also identified as distinguishing factors in her study.

Zimmerman's study of college women who were skilled and

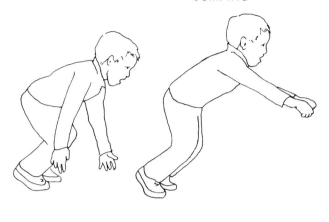

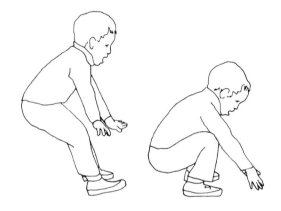

unskilled broad jumpers revealed the persistence of elements of immature form at the adult level.[34] The nonskilled jumpers had limited arm movements and continued to swing their arms sideward as their legs came forward for landing. They did not achieve full extension at takeoff, and they hurried flexion at the hips and knees in the forward swing of the legs during flight. Further, the nonskilled jumpers consistently had larger leg angles at takeoff and at landing. It is apparent from these findings by Halverson and Zimmerman that even in widely separated age groups the poor performers show similar features and degrees of immature form.

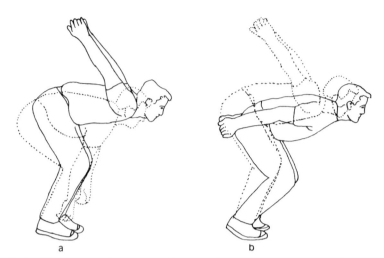

FIG. 4–8. Mature form in the standing long jump prior to takeoff and at landing. Before takeoff: (a) weight moves forward as arms perform preliminary swing; (b) weight continues to move forward as the arms start a downward and forward swing; (c) heels are lifted, arms swing forward and upward, and a series of propulsive forces thrust the body into full extension. Landing: (d) legs are extended and well forward, and trunk and arms are forward in reaction; (e) knees flex when heels contact the ground, and arms and trunk reach forward to prevent a backward fall.

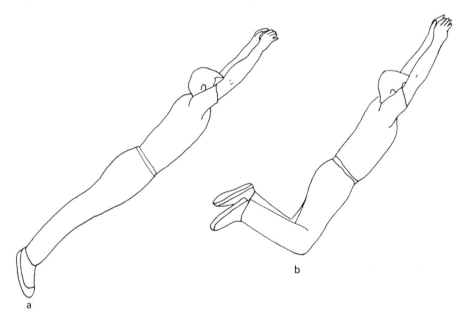

FIG. 4–9. Mature form in the standing long jump during flight: (a) body is fully extended at takeoff; (b) lower legs flex while trunk and arms offer a long lever for reaction; (c) knees come forward as the hips flex and lower legs continue to flex; (d) legs swing forward and begin to extend in preparation for landing, and trunk and arms continue forward and downward in reaction to the leg movement; (e) legs are approximately straight at the knees and reach forward for maximum distance at landing.

76

c   d, e

c   d   e

MATURE FORM IN THE STANDING LONG JUMP

The standing long jump is an explosive flash of closely integrated movements with a distinct underlying pattern (Figs. 4–8; 4–9). In a skillful performance, the following pattern of movements occurs:

1. Joints are cocked by crouching and swinging the arms backward and upward.
2. Arms swing forward and upward and body extension begins in quick succession at the hips, knees, and ankles. (The movements continue until the body is fully extended and off the ground.)
3. Lower legs flex.
4. Hips flex, bringing knees forward, and arms and trunk move forward and downward.
5. Lower legs extend just prior to landing.
6. Knees bend at impact and body weight continues forward and downward in the line of flight.

The Crouch

Since the entire body weight does not have to be lifted directly upward in the standing long jump as it does in the vertical jump, the preparatory crouch can be deeper. The benefit of the deeper crouch is the increased distance provided over which to apply force prior to the takeoff. The 16 male college students studied by Henry were able to crouch an average of 6 inches more in the standing broad jump than in the vertical jump without sacrificing maximum performance.[18] Felton found that the good jumpers among the college women she studied obtained deeper flexion in all the joints involved in the preliminary crouch than that of the poor jumpers.[9] Skilled jumpers automatically seem to assume the amount of crouch that is the most effective for them, considering the strength they have available for propulsion in the jump. Extremes of either depth or shallowness in the crouch do not produce effective propulsion.

The Arm Swing

Several writers have emphasized the importance of the action of the arms in moving the center of gravity of the body forward prior to the takeoff.[4,6,34] The contribution of the arms in performing this task is apparent from the outset of the jump. When the arms swing backward and upward, the forward shift of body weight begins (Fig. 4–8). The forward movement of the body weight continues as the arms change direction and move vigorously downward and forward. During the forward swing the arms remain nearly straight and form a long lever which is useful initially in the development of momentum and later in reaction to leg movement.[26] Flexion at the shoulder continues until the arms are fully extended and in line with the trunk (Fig. 4–9). This position is reached just before takeoff, and when arm movement decelerates the last phase of leg extension can be done against less resistance. The arms remain essentially in line with the trunk, forming a long lever to react against the forward movement of the legs during the flight phase. When the knees are well under the body on the forward swing, the spine flexes slightly, and the arms extend somewhat at the shoulder joint in reaction to the rapid movement of the tucked legs. A continued forward reach of the arms after landing assists in moving the center of gravity forward over the feet for the retention of balance.

Arm action after takeoff is basically compensatory and an alternate form is used by some skilled jumpers. Immediately after the body is airborne, the arms are moved backward to a hyperextended position as the legs are brought forward. Arms are then swung vigorously forward at landing to transfer momentum and carry the center of gravity forward ahead of the two points of support.[8] The double-reversal arm action in this form must be done swiftly. A pseudowinging motion or movement through the high-guard arm position sometimes is used to get the arms into the hyperextended position quickly enough to be effective at landing, but these are not necessarily aspects of immature form.

Average rather than skilled or unskilled long jumpers were studied by Roy et al.[29] Among the 70 subjects were 15 boys in each of age groups 7 and 10, and 20 boys in each of age groups 13 and 16. A force platform was used to determine the kinetic parameters, and a film analysis of the performances of 5 boys in each age group provided data relating to kinematic factors. Roy concluded that the basic kinematics of jumping were well established by the beginning of school age and remained essentially constant through midadolescence. Similarly, the vertical and horizontal force components, although varying in amount from one age to the next, conformed to a general pattern and remained relatively stable over the same age period for average jumpers. The study did not attempt to relate the angular velocity and acceleration measures at the shoulder, hip, knee, ankle, and metatarsal phalangeal joints directly to overt pattern configuration.

Actions at the Hip, Knee, and Ankle Joints Prior to Takeoff

The crouch cocks the hip, knee, and ankle joints by placing them in deeper flexion. There is a minor crouch when the arms swing backward, and the crouch deepens when they swing downward and forward. The heels are pulled off the floor, and the arms begin to move upward to mark the beginning of the sequence of propulsive extension. Extension begins in quick succession at the hip, the knee, and the ankle with an imperceptible time lag before each new action begins. The joints reach full extension immediately after takeoff. Zimmerman's poor performers had simultaneous rather than successive initiation of movement at these joints, and the movements failed to produce complete extension.[34]

The Takeoff Angle

A projectile angle of 45 degrees is theoretically the most effective for producing maximum distance when the initial velocity remains constant. The good jumpers studied by Zimmerman had an average takeoff angle approaching 45 degrees. Characteristically, the better standing long jumpers have a lower takeoff angle. The college men studied by Henry had an average takeoff angle of 41.3 degrees, with a range of 32 to 48 degrees. When the angle is too large, not enough horizontal velocity is produced. If the angle with the horizontal is too small, there is insufficient time to swing the legs through under the body and position them for effective landing. As propulsive force is increased, the angle of takeoff generally is lowered toward the horizontal.

Actions at the Hip, Knee, and Ankle Joints During Flight (Fig. 4–9)

Full body extension is held momentarily after takeoff. Then the lower legs begin to flex, and as they approach an angle of approximately 90 degrees, the thighs also begin to flex. While the knees swing forward, the heels continue to move toward the buttocks. The delay in starting hip flexion tightens the tuck on the forward swing of the legs. A shortened lever created in this way can be moved forward swiftly and with minimal effort. Continued flexion at the hips brings the thigh close to the trunk and permits the lower leg to swing forward into position for landing. The leg is essentially straight at the knee at the moment the heel touches the ground.

The Landing

The effective position for landing is with legs almost straight at the knees and well forward and with the trunk close to the thighs (Fig. 4–8). The closeness of the trunk and thighs keeps the center of gravity high, but forward, and allows the legs to reach forward for maximum distance without heightening the danger of falling backward when landing. The angle of the legs with the ground is 45 degrees or less in skilled jumpers and the angle generally coincides with the in-flight path of the center of gravity.[8] The instant the foot has purchase with the ground, there is flexion at the knees that permits a continued and uninterrupted movement of the body weight down its line of flight. Arms reach forward to help keep the center of gravity moving forward and downward.

DEVELOPMENTAL FORM IN THE RUNNING LONG JUMP

The running long jump, as its name implies, is a combination of two basic skills, running and jumping. Following a fast but moderately short approach run, the jumper takes off into flight from one foot, and then lands on both feet simultaneously. Effective coordination of the run and the jump is difficult, especially when the takeoff spot is specified and the coordination problem is made even more complex by the tendency of the body to rotate forward at takeoff.

Some children can perform the running long jump before the age of 3 years if they run at less than full speed and are not required to take off from a particular place. Cooper and Glassow described the rapid adjustment made by a 33-month-old boy when he was asked to clear an obstacle in his path while running.[6] On his first attempt he took off from one foot and landed on the obstacle with both feet. Next he stepped on and took off from the obstacle, and on his third try he successfully cleared the rolled mat and landed on both feet. These uninstructed attempts show one child's approach to the solution of the problem. He might just as well have used a form Wilson observed in her study of the development of jumping form.[33] The preschool children who were not successful in performing the running long jump took off from one foot and landed on the other, using a typical leap.

Wilson did not find much uniformity or consistency in the form used by 4½- to 12-year-old children when they did the running long jump. Boys were superior to the girls in performance and probably achieved the better jumps because of their faster approach rates. The angle of takeoff and the angle of landing tended to decrease with age, but no other clear-cut trends emerged from the study. Arm action was extremely inconsistent, and in-flight leg action was either a pendular swing or a hurdling action with the trunk in a vertical position (Fig. 4–10).

FIG. 4–10. Running long jump form used by an 11-year-old boy. The angle with the horizontal is high at take-off and at landing. Arm opposition helps his in-flight adjustments.

Additional information on the developmental form used in the running long jump is important to the understanding of intraskill as well as interskill development. However, it is unlikely that there will be much success in studying the skill until the standard testing approach which requires a designated takeoff board is modified drastically or abandoned entirely.

MECHANICAL PRINCIPLES RELATED TO JUMPING

Several mechanical principles apply to the various forms of jumping. The following principles are arranged to coincide with the sequence of movements in the basic pattern of jumping.

1. Additional linear and angular velocity may be gained by increasing the distance over which force is applied (the preparatory crouch).
2. When several forces are applied in succession, each succeeding force must be applied at the point where the preceding one has made its greatest contribution in imparting velocity (succession of forces to thrust the body into space).
3. The final direction of a moving body is a resultant of the magnitude and direction of all the forces which have been applied (direction of movement at takeoff).
4. For every action there is a reaction that is equal in amount and opposite in direction (adjustments during the flight phase).
5. The shock of landing can be diminished by absorbing it either over a greater distance or over a greater area, or both (give

with legs and slide down line of flight). This principle was not discussed in Chapter 1, but it is highly relevant to skills in the category of jumping.

USE OF THE BASIC PATTERN OF JUMPING IN SPORT SKILLS

Advanced forms of jumping usually are combinations of basic skills. Jumping is combined with catching, running, or striking in the running high jump, the long jump, the volleyball spike, the basketball rebound, and the basketball jump ball. In some of these types of sport skills, jumping is the primary basic skill in the pattern; in others it is an important secondary skill. The specific role of the jump will be apparent as a few of these advanced skill patterns are examined.

Jump Ball in Basketball

A basketball is tossed into the air between two opposing players who compete in an attempt to tap the ball to a teammate when it is in its downward flight. The height of the jump is important, but the timing of the jump with the flight of the ball is the critical aspect of the sport skill. The basic pattern of movements is almost identical to the pattern used in the jump and reach. Only the arm movement that controls the direction of the tap is variable. In Figure 4–5, the player crouches, lifts his arms to begin the jump, quickly extends at hips, knees, and ankles, and uses arm opposition to raise his tapping hand as high as possible. His basic jumping pattern must be effective, and his timing must permit him to reach the ball at the peak of his jump. These are essential in the successful use of the skill.

Volleyball Spike

The jump is but one of three basic skills that are combined in the volleyball spike. A short run precedes the jump, and a striking motion follows it. The function of the jump is to gain height so that the ball can be struck in such a way that it crosses the net in a sharply downward trajectory. The movements in the pattern must be timed precisely in relation to the flight of the ball. Two or three running steps toward the net build up momentum for added height in the jump and move the spiker into the correct takeoff position slightly behind the downward trajectory of the ball. A two-footed takeoff is used by the spiker because with this form of vertical jump he can get more upward thrust and can coordinate his arms more effectively after the takeoff. The pattern for the jump that follows the preliminary forward steps is seen in Figure 4–11. The spiker's trunk remains

FIG. 4–11. The volleyball spike. The total skill pattern includes a short run, a jump from a two-footed take-off, and a hit. The arms initiate the jump and then quickly adjust for the spiking motion.

upright as he crouches and swings his arms forward. He begins the jump with the upward lift of his arms and there is extension at the hips, knees, and ankles prior to takeoff. The arms contribute to the balance and general coordination of the jump and then continue to move into position for the striking motion that is the climax of the complex pattern. As in the jump ball in basketball, the timing of the jump in relation to the flight of the ball is a critical factor in the performance of the skill.

Running High Jump

The basic pattern of the jump is present in this complex skill, but all aspects of it are not so readily apparent as they are in other sport skills involving jumping. Attention normally seems to focus on the technique for clearance of the bar and not on the upward thrust that contains the basic pattern. The movements producing the upward thrust are isolated for consideration in Figure 4–12. The sequence emphasizes the unique one-footed

FIG. 4–12. Running high jump. A one-footed take-off necessitates strong upward lift from the arms and the lead leg.

takeoff of the running high jump. The jumper leans backward as he plants his takeoff foot well in front of his center of gravity. The forward momentum he develops during the preliminary run is carried forward and upward over his firmly planted and slightly bent takeoff leg. He swings his lead leg forward quickly with a bent knee and then straightens the leg as it joins the arms in a vigorous lifting motion. Cooper stressed the need to keep the takeoff foot on the ground long enough for the arms and swinging leg to "contribute transference of momentum."[5] Extension of his support leg at the hip, knee, and ankle continues the upward lift and provides the final force for the jump. The jumper's pattern includes a slight crouch, and upward lift from the arms and a final thrust from the support leg. The appearance of this basic jumping pattern is obscured partly by the vigorous lift and high position of the forward leg at takeoff.

ANALYSIS OF FORM IN JUMPING

Jumps are ballistic movements that occur rapidly. Direct visual analysis of a jumper's form in live performance must be based upon observations made during several jumps performed with maximum effort. Attention should be focused upon what seem to be the determinable features of the jumping pattern.

Experience has shown that the following pattern elements can be seen and are extremely valuable in the general analysis of form in jumping.

Vertical Jump

1. Feet are nearly parallel and not more than shoulder width apart in the ready stance.
2. Knees are bent to about a right angle, and the trunk is only slightly forward in the preparatory crouch.
3. Body is in full extension from head to toes at takeoff.

FIG. 4–13. Vertical jump by a 7-year-old boy.

FIG. 4–14. Vertical jump by a 4-year-old boy.

FIG. 4–15. Standing long jump by a 10-year-old girl.

Arm action in the vertical jump is task-oriented, but the arms are not greatly hyperextended during the crouch regardless of their specific task after takeoff.

Standing Long Jump

1. Full body extension from toes through arms at takeoff.
2. Body angle near 45 to 50 degrees with the horizontal at takeoff.
3. Legs out in front of the body with feet parallel at landing.
4. Body slides forward down the line of flight at landing.

Each of these observable items allows several aspects of the pattern of jumping to be evaluated in a single check. Problems in timing and movement coordination, for example, can be picked up in the failure of the body to be in full extension at takeoff. Figures 4–1 (upper), 4–3, 4–4, 4–6, 4–7, 4–13, 4–14, and 4–15 should be studied carefully for trends and stages before the quick analysis items are applied. The final step in direct analysis is actual experience in observing and evaluating the form of live jumpers.

BIBLIOGRAPHY

1. Bangerter, B. L.: Contributive components in the vertical jump. Res. Q. Am. Assoc. Health Phys. Educ., *39*:432, 1968.
2. Bayley, N.: The development of motor abilities during the first three years. Monogr. Soc. Res. Child Dev., *1*:1, 1935.
3. Bleisweiss, G. A.: Relationship of Force Exerted on the Takeoff of the Standing Broad Jump to Strength, Weight, and Distance Jumped. Unpublished Master's Thesis, University of California at Berkeley, 1964.
4. Broer, M.: Efficiency of Human Movement. Philadelphia, W. B. Saunders Co., 1973.
5. Cooper, J. M.: Kinesiology of high jumping. *In* Medicine and Sport, Vol. 2, Biomechanics (Wartenweiler, Jokl, and Hebbelinck, eds.). Baltimore, University Park Press, 1968.
6. Cooper, J., and Glassow, R.: Kinesiology. St. Louis, C. V. Mosby Co., 1972.
7. Couper, M.: An Analysis of the Transfer of Horizontal Momentum to a Vertical Jump. Unpublished Master's Thesis, Smith College, 1965.
8. Dyson, G.: The Mechanics of Athletics. London, University of London Press, 1970.
9. Felton, E.: A Kinesiological Comparison of Good and Poor Jumpers in the Standing Broad Jump. Unpublished Master's Thesis, University of Wisconsin, 1960.
10. Glassow, R. B., Halverson, L. E., and Rarick, G. L.: Improvement of Motor Development and Physical Fitness in Elementary School Children. Cooperative Research Project No. 696, University of Wisconsin, 1965.
11. Gutteridge, M. V.: A study of motor achievements of young children. Arch. Psychol., *244*:1, 1939.
12. Haldeman, N.: A Cinematographical Analysis of the Standing High Jump as Related to the Basketball Jump Ball Situation. Unpublished Master's Thesis, Pennsylvania State University, 1958.

13. Halverson, L. E.: A Comparison of the Performance of Kindergarten Children in the Take-Off Phase of the Standing Broad Jump. Unpublished Doctoral Dissertation, University of Wisconsin, 1958.
14. Halverson, L. E., Roberton, M. A., and Harper, C. J.: Current research in motor development. J. Res. Dev. Educ., *6*:(3) 56, 1973.
15. Hay, J.: Biomechanical aspects of jumping. *In* Exercise and Sport Sciences Reviews: Vol. III (Wilmore and Keogh, eds.). New York, Academic Press, 1975.
16. Heess, R.: Effects of Arm Position and Knee Flexion on Vertical Jumping Performance. Unpublished Master's Problem, Pennsylvania State University, 1964.
17. Hellebrandt, F. A., Rarick, G. L., Glassow, R., and Carns, M. L.: Physiological analysis of basic motor skills: I. Growth and development of jumping. Am. J. Phys. Med., *40*:14, 1961.
18. Henry, C.: Mechanical Analysis of the Initial Velocity in the Sargent Jump and in the Standing Broad Jump. Unpublished Master's Thesis, University of Iowa, 1948.
19. Jenkins, L. M.: A Comparative Study of Motor Achievements of Children Five, Six, and Seven Years of Age. New York, Teachers College, Columbia University, 1930.
20. Johnson, B.: An Analysis of the Mechanics of the Take-Off in the Standing Broad Jump. Unpublished Master's Thesis, University of Wisconsin, 1957.
21. Keogh, J.: Motor Performance of Elementary School Children. Department of Physical Education, University of California, Los Angeles, 1965.
22. Klissouras, V., and Karpovich, P. V.: Electrogoniometric study of jumping events. Res. Q. Am. Assoc. Health Phys. Educ., *38*:41, 1967.
23. Lewis, B.: The Relationship of Selected Factors to the Vertical Jump. Unpublished Master's Thesis, University of Iowa, 1959.
24. Martin, T. P., and Stull, G. A.: Effects of various knee angle and foot spacing combinations on performance in the vertical jump. Res. Q. Am. Assoc. Health Phys. Educ., *49*:324, 1969.
25. McCaskill, C. L., and Wellman, B. L.: A study of common motor achievements at the pre-school ages. Child Dev., *9*:141, 1938.
26. Payne, A. H., Slater, W. J., and Telford, T.: The use of a force platform in the study of athletic activities. Ergonomics, *11*:123, 1968.
27. Poe, A.: Description of the movement characteristics of two-year-old children performing the jump and reach. Res. Q. Am. Assoc. Health Phys. Educ., *47*:260, 1976.
28. Poe, A.: Development of Vertical Jump Skill in Children. Unpublished Study, University of Wisconsin, 1970.
29. Roy, B., Youm, Y., and Roberts, E. M.: Kinematics and kinetics of the standing long jump in 7-, 10-, 13-, and 16-year-old boys. *In* Medicine and Sport, Biomechanics III (Cerquiglini, Venerando, and Wartenweiler, eds.). Basel, Karger, 1973.
30. Scott, M. G.: Analysis of Human Motion. New York, Appleton-Century-Crofts, 1963.
31. Waterland, J. C.: Integration of movement. *In* Medicine and Sport, Vol. II, Biomechanics (Wartenweiler, Jokl, and Hebbelinck, eds.). Baltimore, University Park Press, 1968.
32. Willson, K.: The Relative Effects of Various Foot Spacings on Performance in the Vertical Jump. Unpublished Master's Thesis, Pennsylvania State University, 1965.
33. Wilson, M.: Development of Jumping Skill in Children. Unpublished Doctoral Dissertation, University of Iowa, 1945.
34. Zimmerman, H. M.: Characteristic likenesses and differences between skilled and non-skilled performance of the standing broad jump. Res. Q. Am. Assoc. Health Phys. Educ., *27*:352, 1956.

5

THROWING

Any movement sequence that involves thrusting an object into space by the use of one or two arms technically fits into the general category of throwing. The term has been applied by popular usage to so many different skills that its precise meaning is easily muddled. In this presentation, a mature or skilled throw is considered to be a closely integrated movement sequence that is initiated by a forward step with the contralateral leg, followed by hip and trunk rotation, and concluded with a whipping action of the propelling arm. Although this definition allows overarm, sidearm and underhand motions, the unilateral overarm version is of primary concern here because it is the most commonly used form and it has been studied extensively at both developmental and mature levels.

Many different patterns of throwing appear in the developmental stage, especially at the beginning. Therefore, it is necessary to accept a broad definition of minimal form in order to include the variety of possibilities that mark progress toward the mature pattern. For the purposes of this chapter, minimal throwing form will be considered to be any pattern in which an object is thrust into space cleanly with a unilateral or a bilateral pushing, slinging, tossing, or whipping arm motion.

THROWING PERFORMANCES OF CHILDREN

The development of throwing ability has been the subject of serious study for several decades. There is a substantial accumulation of evidence showing general improvement in throwing ability from late infancy on through childhood. Since the bulk of the research has concentrated on the performances of school age children, the nature of the improvement for that group can be stated more specifically. The trend in performance for elementary school children is toward annual improvement for both boys and girls, with the average performance of boys exceeding the average performance of girls at each grade level.

Form, accuracy, distance, and velocity at release have been used as criteria for evaluating the throwing ability of children. Because of the lack of objectivity involved in rating, form has been the least popular criterion used. In one of the infrequent uses of form, Gutteridge devised a ten-point rating scale and used it to evaluate throwing ability in her study of the motor ability of young children.[12] No child at age 2 or 3 years was rated as being proficient, but there were indications of a progressive increase in the percentage of children who were rated as proficient at ages 4, 5, and 6 years. The assigned ratings represented a wide range of ability at each age level. Although 85% of the children were rated proficient in the age group 5½ to 6 years, the range of ratings for that group extended from excellent down to awkward.

When accuracy is used as the standard for measuring throwing ability, investigators are troubled by not being able to use the same test for children of all ages. The recourse has been to modify the distance from which the ball is thrown, for different age levels at 2- or 3-year intervals. This procedure has the disadvantage of producing a break in the data each time the testing procedure is changed. The result is a sketchy notion of the development of accuracy in throwing, but the limited evidence on accuracy is worthy of brief consideration. In his comprehensive study of the motor achievements of children, Keogh limited the target throw for accuracy to children at ages 7, 8, and 9.[17] He found an improvement in performance and a superiority of boys over girls at each of the three age levels. Wester in an earlier but more comprehensive study, compared the throwing accuracy of 232 boys in grades 3, 4, and 5.[29] The boys threw a baseball, a softball, and a volleyball at a target from distances of 20, 30, and 40 feet. Wester found a progression in mean total scores from grade 3 to grade 4 and from grade 4 to grade 5. Moreover, the subjects were more accurate from the shorter distances and with the two smaller balls. A more recent study supplied results that were similar to those from the earlier research. Among the 960 boys and girls ages 6, 7, 8, and 9 years, there was annual improvement in a throwing-for-accuracy task, and the boys were significantly better than the girls at each age level.[28]

The most frequently encountered criterion for determining throwing ability is the throw for distance. Unfortunately, the many differences in testing procedures deny a direct comparison of the data from the numerous studies in which the throw for distance was used. Despite procedural differences, a strongly defined developmental trend has appeared in the literature. The more recent studies using large numbers of children are consistently in agreement and firmly support the general trend of yearly improvement observed in many of the earlier studies. Keogh studied 1171 children and found a linear year-to-year improvement, with the boys throwing significantly farther than the girls at each age level from 5 to 11 years.[17] A similarly comprehensive study was done by Hanson who analyzed her data on 2840 children according to school grade rather than chronological age.[14] Her findings of yearly improvement and male superiority parallel those of Keogh and have been supported by the additional studies of Nichols and Van Slooten.[20,28]

The sex difference in throwing ability was dramatized by a comparison of the performances of elementary school boys and college women in the softball throw for distance. Brophy reported that 63 freshmen and sophomore college women threw the softball an average of 65.92 feet, with a range of 28 to 138 feet.[5] When Jones placed these data beside the performances of a group of 64 elementary school boys between the ages of 6½ and 10½ years, the comparison was striking.[16] The boys had an average throw of 63.14 feet, with a low score of 19 feet and a best score of 149 feet. Although no statistical comparison was attempted, the similarity of the ranges and the average performances certainly suggests how far boys are ahead of girls in throwing performance, and further hints at the possible level at which girls tend to plateau in performance.

Velocity at release, a technique used primarily in the Wisconsin studies on motor development, is yet another method of measuring throwing performance. It requires either calculations based upon measurements from film analysis or a special velocimeter which gives an automatic reading that can be converted quickly into a velocity score.[23] In one study in which the film analysis technique of measuring throwing velocity was employed, the results accurately repeated the performance picture presented in studies using the throw for distance.[11] Boys were superior to girls, and both boys and girls showed annual improvement.

DEVELOPMENTAL FORM IN THROWING

Children use many types of throws as they begin to acquire skill in throwing, but there does not seem to be a definite or precise order for the appearance of the types. A study by Jones provides some insight into the matter.[16] She analyzed the throwing patterns of 142 boys and girls ranging between 4½ and 10½ years of age. The children collectively used six different patterns when throwing a softball or a volleyball. Among the patterns were (1) bilateral overhand, (2) bilateral underarm from the front, (3) bilateral underarm from the side, (4) bilateral overarm, (5) unilateral underarm, and (6) unilateral overarm. The pattern a child chose to use was dependent upon his size and age and the size of the ball. Before the age of 8, only 2 boys and 2 girls used a unilateral pattern when throwing the volleyball, but after the age of 9, all boys used a unilateral overhand throw. Unilateral patterns were used exclusively when throwing the smaller ball, with the overhand unilateral pattern being used by 90.6% of the boys but only 68.1% of the girls. These might be regarded as *natural* throwing patterns because Jones had not instructed the children concerning which form to use.

The size of the ball was an important factor in Jones' study and presumably also had a significant bearing on the presence and the persistence of bilateral arm action in the patterns used by the children in a study by Deach.[7] She filmed the techniques children ages 2 through 6 years used to throw a *volleyball*. Of the four stages she found, bilateral arm action was used in the first three. Both arms were still involved at stage 3, but the preferred arm assumed more responsibility in the throw. It was not until the final stage of her developmental sequence that the one-arm overhand pattern with trunk rotation and arm-foot opposition was achieved.

Unilateral Overarm Stages

A definitive study of developmental form in unilateral overarm throwing was done many years ago by Wild.[30] She did a cinematographic analysis of the throwing form of selected normal boys and girls at an age interval of 6 months from 2 to 7 years, and at a yearly interval from age 7 through 12 years. From a meticulous and comprehensive analysis of the data, 6 types of throws were identified, but the number was later reduced to 4 stages and each was associated with throwing development according to a particular age schedule. Subsequent observations by Halverson and Roberton, Seefeldt et al., and others have verified the general patterns but prompt one to believe that the patterns might appear earlier than indicated in the tentative schedule that had been proposed.[22,24]

The impact of Wild's study on research relating to the development of throwing patterns has been so great that the four stages are presented here in detail and are accompanied by illustrations from the original data. The four stages continue to

FIG. 5–1. Stage I. The ball is thrown primarily with forearm extension. The feet remain stationary, and the body does not rotate, but there is a slight forward body sway. (Redrawn from Wild.)

have a high degree of practical value because each is relatively easy to identify on the basis of a few major characteristics.

STAGE I. This primal pattern was observed in children at ages 2 and 3 years. It consists almost exclusively of arm movement and occurs in the anteroposterior plane (Fig. 5–1). In preparation for the throw, the arm is brought either sideward and backward or upward and backward until the hand holding the ball is above the shoulder and the forearm of the throwing arm is flexed and extended backward. At the end of the backward motion of the arm, there is considerable retraction of the shoulders and a slight backward sway of the trunk. The throw consists of a forward and downward swing of the arm with extension of the forearm starting early. Simultaneously the backward sway of the trunk is reduced. The feet do not change position during the throw, and there is no rotation of the body except possibly after release.

STAGE II. Children 3½ to 5 years of age formed the group that demonstrated this basic pattern. It is characterized by a rotatory movement in the horizontal plane (Fig. 5–2). The preparatory motion involves a rotation of the trunk to the right with a sideward and backward swing of the arm until the throwing hand terminates in a position somewhat behind the head, with the elbow well flexed. The arm initiates the throwing motion with a forward swing in a high oblique or a more horizontal plane, and the trunk rotates to the left. The forearm extends anytime prior to the release of the ball with the arm following through in a forward and downward movement. Again the feet are together and do not move during the throw. The addition of the rotatory movement in this pattern provides a greater distance over which to apply force in the throw. It represents an improvement over the first pattern in terms of the leverage that can be applied by the trunk and shoulder girdle.

STAGE III. Typical of the throwing pattern of children ages 5 and 6 was the addition of a same-side forward step during the throw, giving the pattern both anteroposterior and horizontal features (Fig. 5–3). Preliminary movements are similar to those employed in the previous pattern. The feet are together and remain stationary while the trunk rotates to the right and the arm is swung sideward, upward, and backward to a position with the forearm flexed. A forward step with the right foot initiates the throwing motion and is followed by rotation of the trunk to the left and a forward swing of the arm in an oblique or in an essentially horizontal plane. The forearm extends later than in Stage II, and the arm follows through in a forward and downward motion. There is minor evidence of "opening" when

FIG. 5–2. Stage II. Rotatory movement is added to the pattern. During the preparatory movement, the hand is cocked behind the head. Then the trunk rotates to the left, and the throwing arm swings around in an oblique–horizontal plane. (Redrawn from Wild.)

FIG. 5–3. Stage III. A forward step with the leg on the same side of the body as the throwing arm is added to the pattern. The step produces additional forward force for the throw. (Redrawn from Wild.)

the arm is drawn back further as the step is taken. Forward force is added to the throw by the forward shifting of body weight during the step. However, using the foot on the same side of the body for the step limits the range of the backward preparatory movements of the throwing arm and continues to impose the awkward timing seen in the earlier patterns.

STAGE IV. This pattern represents the mature or skilled form and was found commonly among boys 6½ years of age and older and to a lesser extent among girls in the same age range. In the preparatory movements, the weight shifts to the right foot as the trunk rotates to the right and the throwing arm is swung backward and upward (Fig. 5–4). A forward step by the opposite foot is followed by counter clockwise rotation of the trunk, horizontal adduction of the arm, and extension at the elbow. The

FIG. 5–4. Stage IV. In the mature pattern the arm and the trunk rotate backward in preparation for the throw. A contralateral step moves the body weight forward, the hips, trunk, and shoulders rotate to the left, and the arm completes the throwing motion. (Redrawn from Wild.)

contralateral step allows more extensive "opening" and greater differentiation of the movements in the pattern. The major obstacle to the achievement of this stage of throwing by girls seems to be the complex forward arm swing.

Some of Wild's observations connected with the identification of the stages continue to have an impact on the understanding of the nature of motor pattern development. One important observation was concerned with the relationship between stages and trends. She recognized that "overlapping of features into chronologically adjacent types demonstrates emergence of one stage into the next." Although different kinds of trends were noted, "the outstanding trend disclosed by the movement types is change from movements in the anteroposterior plane to movements largely in the horizontal plane, and from an unchanging base of support to a left-foot-step forward."[30] With this monumental work and all its implications as a beginning, the study of stages and trends in throwing development has continued at increasingly more diverse and advanced levels.

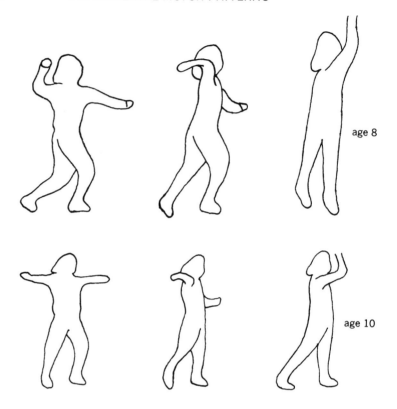

age 8

age 10

FIG. 5–5. Girl filmed while throwing for maximum velocity at ages 8, 9, 10, and 11. At age 8 she was classified as a good thrower based upon the criterion of initial velocity. (Redrawn from Singer.[25])

Age 8. Rotates trunk and cocks arm but restricts trunk rotation by stepping forward on right foot rather than on opposite foot.

Age 9. Little change in form over previous year.

Age 10. Shifts weight forward from right foot to left foot and acquires greater range of movement in shoulder–arm unit. (Evidence of opening.)

Age 11. Good range of motion at all joints but does not extend elbow effectively at the point of release. (Uses a pushing motion.)

A longitudinal study of improvements in the throwing form of a limited number of school girls was done by Singer.[25] Two good and 2 poor throwers were selected on the basis of initial ball velocity, and the 4 girls were filmed at ages 8, 9, 10, and 11 years. Figure 5–5 shows the year-to-year development of the form of one girl who was a *good* performer according to the velocity classification. It is significant to note that at age 8 she continued to manifest the same-side stepping action Wild had identified with 5- and 6-year-old children. At age 10 the subject had

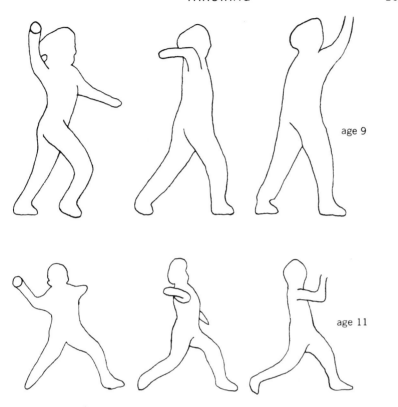

age 9

age 11

abandoned the forward step with the same foot for the more effective opposite-foot-forward pattern. By age 11 she had increased the range of movement at most joints, and her only serious problem was a pushing arm motion in connection with release. There was considerable similarity in the overall patterns of movement for both good and poor performers over the 4-year period, but greater range of joint movement and greater speed of torso and humeral rotation were pinpointed as the factors producing better performance.

Ekern also found that longer stride and greater range of movement characterize better performance.[9] She analyzed the throwing patterns of 2 boys and 2 girls from each of grades 2, 4, and 6 who were the best throwers based upon the measure of ball velocity. The better throwers in the group had greater similarity of body movements, as well as longer steps and greater ranges of motion. With an increase in age, there were increases in forward and lateral trunk inclination at release, and in speed of rotation of the humerus. These changes lead toward acquisition of the flinging arm motion used in the mature pattern. In addition, Ekern detected two sex differences in throwing which help explain the superior performances of boys. Girls showed more variation in arm movements than the boys and they did not have the ability to separate pelvic-spinal rotations.

Changes in movement pattern resulting from instruction in throwing at the kindergarten level were examined critically by Hanson.[15] The throwing patterns of many of the children matured to some extent in several respects: (1) in starting position, change from a narrow front-facing to a wider side-facing position, (2) in trunk rotation, change from "block" rotation to a pelvic-spinal sequence, (3) in arm action, less horizontal adduction of the humerus, and (4) in elbow extension, more delay in starting it. One especially important feature of Hanson's study was her proposal that the development of trunk rotation might follow three stages from pelvis and spine together; to spine, then pelvis; and finally to pelvis, then spine. The first and third stages of trunk rotation are well verified as a proper developmental sequence, but the intermediate spine-then-pelvis stage has not been adequately substantiated.

Other studies have involved an expansion of the number of stages in throwing development.[3,18,22] Leme added 4 patterns to Wild's original 6 in her study of the developmental aspects of throwing in a group of college women who were poor throwers.[18] Foot position, stride, body orientation, weight shift, trunk action, reverse arm movement, forward arm movement, and follow through were the eight components examined in the analysis of each throw. The throwing patterns of almost all the 18 poor throwers fit into one of the categories, and only 2 of the other 10 types even appeared. The stage that most throwers had reached utilized block rotation of the pelvis and spine and a relatively short stride. This immature pattern is easily anticipated because all the college women were throwing with a maximum velocity of less than 50 feet per second.

In a study of the throwing patterns of 110 educable mentally retarded (EMR) children between the ages of 7 and 12 years,

Auxter detected 15 distinguishable patterns.[3] Each represented an improvement in development toward the objective of efficient throwing. He reported that progress in the 15 patterns was consistent with the progress in Wild's 4 basic patterns, but the expanded group of patterns offered more discrimination in the identification of performance level. Auxter also observed that some of the elements of the throw, such as the number of integrated joint actions involved and the length of the stride, appeared to develop independently of one another. This feature of motor pattern development supports the need to consider development in terms of trends as well as in terms of an expanded number of stages.

The greatest expansion of the number of stages in throwing occurred in the recent study of stage stability by Roberton.[22] She designated 5 categories of arm-trunk development as major stages and 8 categories of pelvic-spinal development as steps within the stages. Both stages and steps were ordered in terms of expected level of difficulty. The major stages and steps were then combined into a total of 25 possible minor stages. Each of 73 first grade children in her study was filmed from two views while performing 10 maximum velocity throws. Of the 25 minor stages that had been hypothesized, 18 appeared in the total of 727 throws and 2 which had not been hypothesized were identified and added. However, the throws were not distributed evenly among the minor stages. More than 80% of all throws appeared in one of 5 minor stages and 1% or less of all throws appeared in each of 11 other minor stages. Thirty-eight percent of all the throws by the first grade children fit into the minor stage "humerus oblique: simultaneous initiation of pelvis and spine (block rotation)," which was in the first major stage. Girls were represented only in the easiest two of the major stages, and boys were found in all five. If another feature such as the stride were to be added when hypothesizing stages of throwing development, the number of discrete stages would increase astronomically and the scattering of patterns would undoubtedly be more widespread than was found in the 25 minor-stage model. Roberton carefully placed her approach in perspective by referring to it as a "viable, developmental research paradigm for the overarm throw." Its use in future research will greatly enhance the understanding of motor pattern development.

MATURE PATTERN FOR THE OVERHAND THROW

Plagenhoef defined the throwing motion as "the properly timed coordination of accelerations and decelerations of all body segments in a sequence of action from the left foot to the right hand that produces maximum absolute velocity of the right hand."[21] His concept of the motion is based on a link system of movements starting from the planted left foot, moving upward to the left hip, diagonally across the pelvis and up the trunk to the right shoulder, through the right elbow, and out to the right hand. The proper coordination of movement in this system ultimately produces the whiplike arm action that typifies the mature overarm throw.

The coordination of accelerations and decelerations of body parts referred to by Plagenhoef was clarified by Atwater in a study of the throwing patterns of 5 skilled males, 5 skilled females, and 5 females of average ability.[2] She found that as a segment accelerates, the succeeding segment lags behind before acquiring the speed of the segment(s) moving it, and then quickly accelerates to reach an even greater angular speed as the preceding segment decelerates. In this way there is a buildup in velocity with the action of succeeding segments. Atwater concluded that "the ability to achieve initial ball velocities well above average appears to be directly associated with the thrower's ability to permit decelerating-accelerating motion of each segment to occur in sequence on top of the accelerating-decelerating speed of the preceding segment." The point explains the ineffectiveness of unitary motions such as block rotation.

A capsule description of the basic pattern of movements in the overhand throw is *Step–Turn–Throw*. This triad is a simplification of the movements in a very complex skill, but it helps isolate key points for instructional emphasis and underlines the proper sequence of movements. An outline of the full pattern for a right handed thrower is as follows:

Preparatory Movement
1. The body pivots to the right with the weight on the right foot and the throwing arm swings backward and upward.

Throwing Movements
2. The left foot strides forward in the intended direction of the throw.
3. The hips, then spine, and shoulders rotate counterclockwise as the throwing arm is retracted to the final point of its reversal.
4. The upper arm is rotated medially and then the forearm is extended with a whipping action.
5. And the ball is released.

Follow-Through
6. The pattern of movements is continued until the momentum generated in the throwing action is dissipated.

This sequence is the general pattern of movements in a vigorous, forceful overhand throw. The order of the successive movements in the sequence is quite specific, but there is overlapping in conformance with the accelerating-decelerating principle of segment action. The precise manner in which each of the movements is performed may vary because of the starting position, the purpose of the throw, and individual differences in strength and flexibility, but the sequence remains constant. Moreover, Collins found a remarkable similarity in the basic mechanics of the overarm and sidearm throws.[6] Diagrams of the movements used in the overhand throw by the adult male and the adult female in Collins' study are shown in Figure 5–6. Collins' findings were corroborated by Atwater who also studied the sidearm and overarm throwing patterns of skilled males and females.[1] Her conclusion was that the rate, sequence, and timing for pelvic rotation, spinal rotation, shoulder lateral rotation,

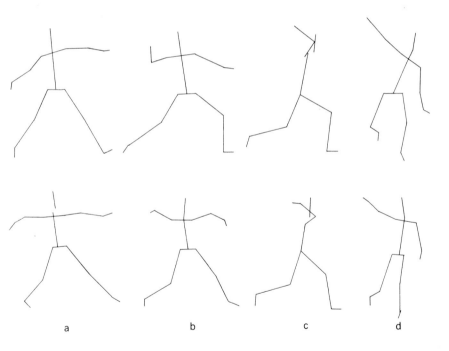

a   b   c   d

FIG. 5–6. Overhand throwing pattern of an adult female (lower) and an adult male (upper); (a) beginning of pelvic rotation, (b) beginning of spinal rotation, (c) beginning of shoulder medial rotation, (d) beginning of wrist flexion (front view). The similarities in the basic movements are evident. The conspicuous lack of lateral flexion in the female (d) is the main difference, and it probably is a result of the restrictive position of her left leg. (Redrawn from Collins.[6])

shoulder medial rotation, and elbow extension were impressively similar for both throws.

THE PREPARATORY MOVEMENT

The preparatory movements contribute to the throw only in the sense that they put the body in a position for the application of effective leverage in the throwing motion. These movements vary considerably from the elaborate ritual used by baseball pitchers during their "windup," to the simple and ineffective backward twisting of the trunk employed by a child who stands in a forward stride position with his opposite foot forward. In preparation for the full overhand throw with maximum effort, the weight shifts to the right leg and the trunk rotates approximately 90 degrees backward to the right. The throwing arm swings backward and somewhat upward, but ordinarily the cocking of the throwing arm is not completed until after the beginning of the throwing motion.

The Forward Stride

The series of forward movements in the throw begins with a stride. Body weight begins to shift forward from the right foot as the left foot strides well forward reaching slightly to the left. By stepping to the left, the thrower places his forward foot so it will allow full effective rotation of his hips during the throw. Forward body movement initiated by the stride continues throughout the throwing motion and is terminated in the follow-through phase of the pattern. Lyon found that the subjects in his study who threw with the greatest velocity continued to flex the trunk at the hip through the point of release (Fig. 5–7).[19] However, the forward leg for each subject was locked at the knee prior to the shoulder–arm action. Although the total body weight is shifted forward with the stride, the lower part of the body is blocked so the link system can develop the whipping action of the arm.

The Trunk Rotation

Just before the left foot touches the ground, the hips start to rotate to the left followed in order by rotation of the spine and shoulders. Body mass continues to move forward during trunk rotation, and the throwing arm reaches its final cocked position in preparation for medial rotation. The added velocity produced by trunk rotation contributes significantly to the speed of the throw. Toyoshima and associates calculated that stride and body rotation contribute 46.9% of the velocity of the throw.[27]

FIG. 5–7. A. Left-handed professional baseball pitcher shown from the top view and from the front view. The sequence is from right to left. The three figures to the left in the top sequence emphasize the whipping action of the forearm in throwing. B. Same pitcher shown from the side view. The sequence is from right to left and from top to bottom. (Redrawn from Lyon.[19])

The Arm Motion

The humerus lags slightly behind a line through the shoulders until the trunk has rotated to the left and the shoulders are nearly perpendicular to the intended direction of the throw. The forward swing that occurs in conjunction with spinal and shoulder girdle rotation should not be confused with either medial rotation or horizontal adduction at the shoulder joint, both of which occur later. While the shoulders are rotating vigorously forward, the forearm is forced backward and downward until it is nearly horizontal and the elbow remains bent at about a right angle. This lateral rotation of the humerus is the final cocking of the arm before the whipping action begins. Then forceful medial rotation at the shoulder starts to swing the forearm forward, and extension at the elbow begins shortly thereafter. Forearm extension causes the elbow to elevate and, along with lateral trunk flexion, raises the arm to an oblique angle above the horizontal. The forearm is still extending at the instant the ball is released, but the arm is nearly straight. Wrist action, which had been accepted as the final and greatest contributor to ball velocity in the overhand throw, is now a controversial feature. Collins reported incredible angular velocity connected with prerelease wrist action, but her findings have not been verified.[6] Dobbins used elgons to measure joint movement and a circuit breaker system to indicate ball release.[8] With his precise procedure, he found that 26 degrees of flexion had occurred at the wrist during forearm extension and the wrist was still in a position of 20 degrees of hyperextension at release. Even Tarbell's analysis of a throw that had been filmed at a camera speed of 1500 frames per second failed to clarify either the matter of wrist action or the question of how the ball leaves the hand.[26]

The point at which the ball is released varies but is approximately even with a lateral plane just in front of the head. The intended angle of release and other factors such as the maturity of the arm action determine the precise point. Those who throw with a whipping or flailing arm motion release the ball near the plane in front of the head; those who are "pushers" release the ball further forward. The distinction between whiplike and pushing arm motions is important for reasons other than the effect on the point of release. It is critical to the understanding of the mature throwing pattern. In the whipping arm action of the mature throw, the forearm is flung into extension faster by the speed acquired in the early movements of the throw than it could be by mere contraction of the triceps muscle. The immature pushing motion is a result of horizontally adducting the arm until the elbow is nearly in front of the shoulder before the forearm is extended. Unfortunately the motion of the arm in the throw is so rapid that it is difficult to analyze in detail, but the gross difference between flailing and extreme pushing can be detected by observation without the use of film. Atwater found that those who use the pushing motion have less total range of motion in their throwing patterns.[2] Besides, the pusher tends to have far less forearm extension at release than the flinger.

The Follow-through

After the ball has been released, the throwing arm continues diagonally downward across the body toward the stable forward support foot. The follow-through is merely an extension of the natural throwing motion which permits deceleration of the throwing arm and assures a smooth and safe finish of the movement.

SELECTED MECHANICAL PRINCIPLES APPLICABLE TO THROWING

Several major mechanical principles are utilized in the basic pattern of the throw. The extent to which some are applicable varies according to the amount of velocity required for the particular throw. When the development of maximum velocity is the objective of the throw, all of the principles listed apply.

1. Additional linear and angular velocity may be gained by increasing the distance over which force is applied (preparatory turn and cocking of the arm).
2. Linear and angular motion must be integrated for optimal performance in many movement patterns (the step-turn sequence).
3. When several forces are applied in succession, each succeeding force must be applied at the point when the preceding one has made its greatest contribution in imparting velocity (succession of forces producing hip, trunk, shoulder, and elbow movements). The acceleration–deceleration of segments reported by Atwater,[2] Plagenhoef and others is typical of the whiplike or linkage motion that produces maximum velocity.[21]
4. The potential linear velocity at the end of a lever is increased by increasing the length of the lever (extension of the forearm in the whipping motion of the arm).

SPORT SKILLS USING THE BASIC PATTERN OF THROWING

The basic mature pattern of throwing is used in a wide variety of sport skills. Each sport skill in the category of throwing has unique aspects and different velocity requirements, but there is common adherence to the basic pattern.

The Sidearm Throw in Baseball

Catching a rolling or bouncing ball and throwing it to first base quickly from an awkward position is a task that must be performed frequently by an infield baseball or softball player. The sidearm throw is used on this and on other similar occasions when a rapid arm action is needed. Finley demonstrated that the sidearm throwing action takes less time than the overhand motion because the arm is not cocked so far back.[10] He also pointed out that the sidearm throw imparts less initial velocity to the ball than the overhand throw. That is not a drawback in this situation because the reduced total amount of time for the throw is a more important factor than the initial velocity of the ball.

The basic throwing pattern emerges clearly in the sidearm form of the player in Figure 5-8. He steps forward, rotates his trunk, cocks his arm, swings his elbow forward, and whips his forearm into extension. Movements in the sidearm throw generally are abbreviated in comparison to the exaggeration of the pitching motion or the throw to home plate from the outfield. Although the amount of body movement in the different forms of throwing used in baseball varies considerably, the same underlying fundamental movement pattern is present in each.

The Football Forward Pass

Stride, turn–cock, and throw. These steps in the fundamental throwing sequence are emphasized vividly in the series of actions in Figure 5-9. The movements are the same as in the

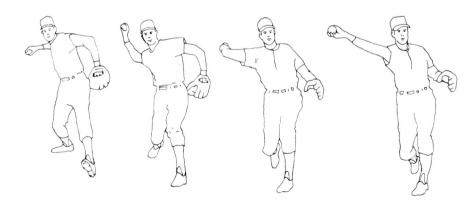

FIG. 5–8. Sidearm throw in baseball.

FIG. 5–9. Forward pass in football.

baseball throw with the exception that the arm motion of the passer is a bit lower than might be expected in the overhand throw. For this sequence of drawings, the football was thrown a distance of just 15 yards at a moderate rate of speed. The action at all joints would have been greater and the ball would have been released at a higher point if the distance of the throw had been 40 or 50 yards.

A distinctive part of the passing pattern is the arm action which is influenced by the size of the ball and by the method of release. The passer in Figure 5–9 carefully keeps his hand behind the ball when his arm is being cocked and then smoothly whips his hand forward so the ball can be spun around its long axis and released without wobbling. The child is particularly aware of the problem of handling the football when learning to pass it. Even when using a junior size ball, he limits his backswing and tends to push the ball ineffectively until he discovers the knack of imparting spin during release.

The Javelin Throw

A grossly exaggerated version of the movements in the overhand throwing pattern is used in the javelin event in track and field athletics. The aim of the throw is to get maximum performance by throwing the javelin as far as possible. The goal of providing maximum effective velocity is apparent from the beginning of the movement. A run helps develop forward momentum, and a pivot or cross step turns the body in preparation for unleashing powerful angular forces. Once the throwing motion begins, it is an unraveling of the fundamental series of movements in the overhand throw, each vigorously delineated. The thrower in Figure 5–10a has been stopped after stepping forward, rotating his hips and trunk and starting the

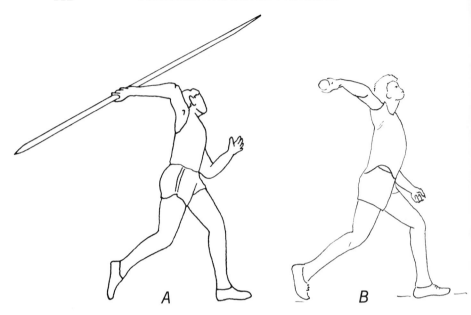

FIG. 5-10.   a. The javelin throw. b. The baseball pitch. Note the similarities and the differences in the body positions in these two sport skills.

forward movement of his throwing arm. This position compares favorably with the exaggerated position used in the overhand baseball pitch (Fig. 5–10b). The noticeable differences in position can be attributed to the greater forward momentum of the javelin thrower and his much higher angle of release.

Overhand Basketball Pass

The overhand basketball pass is another specific sport skill in which the basic pattern of the overhand throw prevails even though maximum ball velocity at release is not the objective. It is demonstrated by the player in Figure 5–11 who takes a forward step, rotates his hips and trunk forward, swings his upper arm medialward, and extends his forearm just before the ball is released. The limitation of the backward swing of the throwing arm that was noted earlier in connection with the football pass is even more necessary in the overhand basketball pass. For most persons, the basketball is too large and too heavy to be controlled by grasping it with one hand so a second hand helps raise the ball into the throwing position. Control of the ball at the end of the backswing is maintained by cradling it in the hand momentarily until forward motion of the arm begins and then lateral rotation of the forearm is limited in the final stage of cocking. These

FIG. 5–11. Overhand basketball pass. The forearm lags during trunk rotation, but the weight of the ball encourages pushing more than whipping arm action.

adjustments limit the effective range of arm movement and interfere with the production of a whiplike motion.

The amount of backswing of the throwing arm in the overhand basketball pass varies according to the size, strength, and skill of the thrower. Children and unskilled players find the basketball truly an unwieldy object and tend to use more of a push than a throw in the final phase of arm action. Girls often turn to the sidearm slinging motion when throwing the basketball for maximum distance because with this form they have improved leverage and a greater distance over which to develop velocity. However, when the throw must be accurate as well as far, the girls return to the overhand throwing pattern.

ANALYSIS OF FORM IN THROWING

There are two features of a high-velocity throw that are exceedingly difficult to analyze precisely by direct visual observation. One feature is the sequence of trunk rotation and the other is the throwing motion of the arm. Since both occur very quickly, direct visual analysis must depend more upon secondary than upon primary information. Some general aspects of the throwing pattern which provide critical secondary information for dealing with trunk and arm action are:

1. Preparatory turning of the trunk away from the intended direction of the throw.
2. A long forward stride with the opposite foot.

3. "Opening" of the pattern by backward movement of the shoulder and throwing arm during the step.
4. Vigorous whipping action of the arm. (A detectable hitch in the continuity of the arm motion characterizes the immature "pushing" motion.)

The first two of the four items can be checked in a single throw, but the other two movement characteristics usually require observation of several throws, including observations from posterior and lateral views. The posterior view provides an important perspective for the detection of backward arm action in "opening" and for checking to determine whether foot placement in the stride allows or restricts trunk rotation.

Attempts at analysis of throwing should begin at a simple level with the four stages described by Wild. They are reasonably clear-cut and can be applied easily and effectively. Review of Figures 5–1, 5–2, 5–3, and 5–4 should precede stage analysis of the sequences in Figures 5–5, 5–12, 5–13, 5–14, and 5–15. When confidence has been gained in the use of the stages, more precise analysis of trunk and arm movements can be attempted. The experience of analyzing the sequences previously mentioned will serve to sharpen observation in preparation for analysis of live throwing, which is a highly challenging task.

FIG. 5–12. Throwing pattern of a 4-year-old boy.

FIG. 5–13. Throwing pattern of a 9-year-old girl.

FIG. 5–14. Throwing pattern of a 4½-year-old boy.

FIG. 5–15. Throwing pattern of a 7-year-old boy.

BIBLIOGRAPHY

1. Atwater, A. E.: Cinematographic Analysis of Overarm and Sidearm Throwing Patterns. AAHPER Research Paper, 1968.
2. Atwater, A. E.: Movement Characteristics of the Overarm Throw: A Kinematic Analysis of Men and Women Performers. Unpublished Doctoral Dissertation, University of Wisconsin, 1970.
3. Auxter, D.: Throwing Patterns of the Mentally Retarded. Research Abstracts. AAHPER, Washington, D. C., 1973.
4. Bowne, M.: Relationship of selected measures of acting body levers to ball throwing velocities. Res. Q. Am. Assoc. Health Phys. Educ., *31*:392, 1960.
5. Brophy, K.: A Kinesiological Study of the Improvement in Motor Skill. Unpublished Master's Thesis, University of Wisconsin, 1948.
6. Collins, P.: Body Mechanics of the Overarm and Sidearm Throws. Unpublished Master's Thesis, University of Wisconsin, 1960.
7. Deach, D.: Genetic Development of Motor Skills of Children Two Through Six Years of Age. Unpublished Doctoral Dissertation, University of Michigan, 1950.
8. Dobbins, D. A.: Loss of Triceps on an Overarm Throw for Speed. Unpublished Master's Thesis, University of Wisconsin, 1970.
9. Ekern, S. R.: An Analysis of Selected Measures of the Overarm Throwing Patterns of Elementary School Boys and Girls. Unpublished Doctoral Dissertation, University of Wisconsin, 1969.

10. Finley, R.: Kinesiological Analysis of Human Motion. Unpublished Doctoral Thesis, Springfield College, 1961.
11. Glassow, R. B., Halverson, L. E., and Rarick, G. L.: Improvement of Motor Development and Physical Fitness in Elementary School Children. Cooperative Research Project No. 696, University of Wisconsin, 1965.
12. Gutteridge, M. V.: A study of motor achievements of young children. Arch. Psychol., 244:1, 1939.
13. Halverson, L. E., and Roberton, M. A.: A Study of Motor Pattern Development in Young Children. Report to National Convention of AAHPER, Chicago, 1966.
14. Hanson, M.: Motor Performance Testing of Elementary School Age Children. Unpublished Doctoral Dissertation, University of Washington, 1965.
15. Hanson, S.: A Comparison of the Overhand Throw Performance of Instructed and Non-Instructed Kindergarten Boys and Girls. Unpublished Master's Thesis, University of Wisconsin, 1961.
16. Jones, F.: A Descriptive and Mechanical Analysis of Throwing Skills of Children. Unpublished Master's Thesis, University of Wisconsin, 1951.
17. Keogh, J.: Motor Performance of Elementary School Children. Department of Physical Education, University of California, Los Angeles, March 1965.
18. Leme, S. A.: Developmental Throwing Patterns in Adult Female Performers Within a Selected Velocity Range. Unpublished Master's Thesis, University of Wisconsin, 1973.
19. Lyon, W.: A Cinematographical Analysis of the Overhand Baseball Throw. Unpublished Master's Thesis, University of Wisconsin, 1961.
20. Nichols, B.: A Comparison of Two Methods of Developing the Overhand Throw for Distance in Four, Five, Six, and Seven Year Old Children. Unpublished Doctoral Dissertation, University of Iowa, 1971.
21. Plagenhoef, S.: Patterns of Human Motion: A Cinematographic Analysis. Englewood Cliffs, N. J., Prentice-Hall, Inc., 1971.
22. Roberton, M. A.: Stability of Stage Categorizations Across Trials: Implications for the 'Stage Theory' of Overarm Throw Development. Unpublished Doctoral Dissertation, University of Wisconsin, 1975.
23. Roberts, T. W.: Incident light velocimetry. Percept. Mot. Skills, 34:263, 1972.
24. Seefeldt, V., Reuschlein, S., and Vogel, P.: Sequencing Motor Skills Within the Physical Education Curriculum. Paper presented at AAHPER Meeting, Houston, 1972.
25. Singer, F.: Comparison of the Development of the Overarm Throwing Patterns of Good and Poor Performers (Girls). Unpublished Master's Thesis, University of Wisconsin, 1961.
26. Tarbell, T.: Some Biomechanical Aspects of the Overhand Throw. Proceedings of the C. I. C. Symposium on Biomechanics (Cooper, ed.), Athletic Institute, Chicago, 1971.
27. Toyoshima, S., Hoshikawa, T., Miyashita, M., and Oguri, T.: Contribution of the body parts to throwing performance. In Biomechanics IV (Nelson and Morehouse, eds.). Baltimore, University Park Press, 1974.
28. Van Slooten, P.: Performance of Selected Motor-Coordination Tasks by Young Boys and Girls in Six Socio-Economic Groups. Unpublished Doctoral Dissertation, Indiana University, 1973.
29. Wester, B.: A Comparison of the Accuracy of Throwing of Third, Fourth, and Fifth Grade Boys. Unpublished Master's Thesis, University of Iowa, 1939.
30. Wild, M.: The behavior pattern of throwing and some observations concerning its course of development in children. Res. Q. Am. Assoc. Health Phys. Educ., 9(3):20, 1938.

6

CATCHING

Catching is a fundamental skill that involves the use of the hand(s) and/or other parts of the body to stop and control an aerial ball or object. The broadness of this definition makes it more applicable to minimal form than to mature form because of its permissiveness toward the use of multiple body parts in the act of catching. Hand-catching seems to be the accepted version for mature form in this skill category. It has been the criterion for evaluating the effectiveness and efficiency of technique in most research on catching and is used almost exclusively in sports where ball-catching is a major skill. When other body segments are used in conjunction with the hands, the act becomes a form of trapping: i.e., the ball is clutched to the chest or trunk with help from arms and hands. In this chapter, various forms of trapping will be considered minimal form, but only hand-catching of aerial balls will be regarded as mature form.

CATCHING PERFORMANCE OF CHILDREN

Proficiency in catching seems to be developed at a comparatively slow rate, but precise evidence concerning its emergence is inconclusive. Observation of the catching behavior of children ages 18 months to 8 years led Seefeldt to conclude that success in catching a ball is possible for 2- and 3-year-old children.[8] The success to which he referred, presumably, is at a primitive level (Stage 1 or 2, page 129). Sinclair found evidence of success at an early age when trapping types of catching were used but saw little indication of active use of hands in the catching patterns of young children.[11]

Gutteridge reported that 56% of 78 five-year-old children and 63% of 67 six-year-old children were proficient catchers.[3] By contrast, 80% of the 5-year-old children in her study were rated

119

as proficient throwers. These figures point up the well-known fact that children learn to throw more quickly than they learn to catch. Despite the evident difficulty of learning to catch, both boys and girls tend to show improvement in catching skill each year and at successive grade levels in the elementary school. The improvement trends are based upon success in catching increasingly smaller balls and upon greater effectiveness when using hand-catching technique.

Catching behavior is difficult to study because of the number of variables influencing the measurement of performance. Major variables are (1) the size of the ball, (2) the distance the ball travels before it is caught, (3) the method of projecting the ball, (4) the direction of the ball in relation to the catcher, (5) the speed of the ball, (6) the precatch change of position required, and (7) the arm-hand action of the catcher. The difficulty of measuring catching performance is abundantly clear from the scarcity of reported studies. A few details from some of the studies on catching will illustrate the variety of procedures and findings.

Hoadley constructed a throwing machine capable of projecting a ball 16 feet and used balls of three different sizes in her study of the catching ability of 250 elementary school children in grades 1 through 4.[6] She found that boys and girls improved in the ability to catch large and small balls at successive grades, with the most significant increases coming between grades 2 and 3 for both sexes. At the first grade level there was no sex difference in catching balls of any size, and at grades 2 and 3 there was no sex superiority in catching the large ball. Boys in this study were able to catch a small ball better than girls in grades 2, 3, and 4.

A hoop-controlled ball catch was used by Seils to measure the catching ability of 510 primary school children.[10] The tennis ball traveled 10 linear feet or less and through a controlling hoop before being caught. On the basis of this relatively simple test, Seils found improvement at successive grade levels, with boys showing better average performances at grades 1 and 2, and girls presenting a higher average score at grade 3.

The distance the ball traveled before being caught was increased in Warner's study of the motor ability of 841 third, fourth, and fifth grade boys.[14] A ball was tossed to the catcher at chest height from a distance of 20 feet. Five trials were given with a volleyball and five with a tennis ball. Five catches out of five attempts with the volleyball were scored by 70.1% of the third grade boys, 84.6% of the fourth grade boys, and 92.5% of the fifth grade boys. No one failed to make at least one catch with the larger ball. A perfect score on five attempts with a tennis ball was made respectively by 57.5%, 78.5%, and 87.2% of the third, fourth, and fifth graders. The only total failures with the tennis ball were by less than 1% of the third grade boys.

A different approach to the study of catching performance was used more recently by Bruce.[1] He varied the trajectory and velocity of the ball and in several experimental conditions required the catcher to move in preparation for catching. A ball-throwing machine controlled the projection of the tennis balls that were used, and each catching attempt was rated on a carefully devised 5-point scale. The subjects were 480 children equally divided between boys and girls and among grades 2, 4, and 6. His findings verified both the expected improvement of performance with advancing grade level and the anticipated superiority of the catching ability of boys. The results showing the effects of precatch change of position and increased ball velocity on performance are of special interest. Performance was not adversely affected when lateral movement was required prior to catching. The children encountered substantial difficulty, however, when it was necessary to adjust by moving forward or backward. The performance of children in the second and fourth grades also deteriorated when the velocity of the ball was increased. Since the sixth-grade children were not bothered by the increase in the speed of the ball, Bruce suggested the possibility of a critical value for velocity beyond which catching performance is impaired. This study was particularly significant because it reached into the relatively unopened bag of problems connected with advanced catching skill. Adjustive movement, height of ball trajectory, and ball velocity are factors most certainly related to comprehensive catching skill, but none has been studied extensively.

Adjustive movement was a major feature in Pederson's (1973) investigation of the catching behavior of 600 first, third, and fifth grade children. Eleven relatively simple catching tasks were devised, including a variety of situations requiring the child to catch an aerial ball before or after it bounced and with or without precatch adjustive movement. An 8½-inch playground ball was rolled off a special piece of apparatus from a height of 12 feet either directly toward the floor or toward a rebound board located on a low platform. Each attempt was scored on a 5-point scale which ranged from a noncontact miss (0) to an unbobbled catch (4). Catching ability, as measured by Pederson, improved significantly for the children in each of the successive grades included in the study. Boys were more successful than girls in grades 1 and 3, but there was no difference in performance at grade 5. The generally high level of success in the catching tasks could be attributed to the simplicity of the tasks and/or tester control of the start of precatch movement which minimized the inevitable problems of timing.

Catching performance as measured by the ability to make a judgment concerning the flight of the ball and then move into effective catching position was the subject of a study by Williams.[17] She was more concerned about the preparatory judgments and adjustive movements than she was with the mechanics of stopping and controlling the ball. In her study, a Ballboy projected a tennis ball in a 34- or a 44-degree trajectory, at a fast or a slow velocity, to one of six predetermined positions. The positions were directly forward or backward or diagonally forward or backward to the left or to the right. Williams' 54 subjects included 9 skilled and 9 unskilled male players from the junior high school, the senior high school, and the college levels. She found the skilled more than twice as accurate as the unskilled in judging the flight of the ball. When the ball moved directly toward the performer, he judged it more accurately than when it was to his right or to his left. For the group as a whole, the 44-degree trajectory was easier to judge, but for the unskilled, judgments were more accurate for balls projected at a 34-degree angle. The latter finding is an extension of the common observation that unskilled catchers of elementary school age have more difficulty judging a ball with a high angle of trajectory than one with a low angle. Apparently the velocity of the ball movement in this study was not critical enough to be a distinguishing factor nor was the variability of the ages of the subjects. If the subjects had been younger and less experienced, Williams undoubtedly would have learned much more about precatch judgments and movements.

Catching performance is dependent partly upon the effectiveness with which visual cues are used. Torres studied the relationship between figure-ground perceptual ability and ball catching ability in 10- and 13-year-old boys and girls.[12] She found no sex differences in ground-figure perceptual ability at either age level, but both sexes in the older group were better in this visual perceptual ability. The test of ball catching ability consisted of making the spatial adjustments necessary for catching when the ball approached at different angles. Boys in both age groups were superior to girls in making the necessary spatial adjustments, and the older group was significantly better than the younger group. However, figure-ground perceptual ability had only a slight positive relationship to catching ability as measured in the study. Other visual abilities apparently are more important in catching performance.

Hellweg analyzed the perceptual and performance characteristics of the catching skill of the best and the poorest of a group of 6- to 7-year-old children.[5] The 10 best and the 10 poorest catchers were selected on the basis of ratings by three judges who used a 5-point scale. The two groups were tested and found to have equally mature visual systems. They were also tested on the ability to judge the path of an approaching ball and indicate when it arrived at a predetermined point, and again there was no significant difference between the groups. The test of catching performance utilized a soft, fleece-covered ball 4 inches in diameter that was projected a distance of 15 feet before arriving at the catcher. The major visual difference between the groups was that the successful catchers appeared to track the ball until it was contacted, whereas the nonsuccessful catchers closed their eyes prior to contact. Nonvisual factors differentiating the groups were: (1) successful catchers initiated movement toward the ball earlier, and (2) successful catchers were starting to give with the ball at contact rather than continuing to reach for it as the nonsuccessful group did.

Hellweg's finding relative to the importance of watching the ball is consistent with the results of a study by Whiting et al.[15,16] Whiting's group varied the amount of time an in-flight ball could be seen before it had to be caught. As the opportunity for watching the ball increased, the catching success of the 36 adult male subjects also increased. Subsequently Whiting concluded that a skilled catcher who has learned the flight characteristics of a ball does not need to keep his eye on the ball during its entire flight. However, the less skilled the catcher is, the more important it is for him to watch the entire trajectory.

It is apparent from the research that relatively little is known about many of the factors involved in catching behavior. In fact, the more difficult aspects of catching performances have been barely illuminated by study of the judgments and movements required in successful performance. Much research remains to be done.

DEVELOPMENT OF SKILL IN CATCHING

The child's first important precatching experience requires him to deal with a rolling ball. He may sit with his legs spread and, when a ball is rolled slowly toward his central axis, attempt to grasp it or try to trap it against one of his legs. Controlling a ball rolled directly at him at a slow rate of speed is his easiest and earliest catching-related experience. Virtually no adjustment is required because the ball moves only in the horizontal plane. The child merely has to time his grasping or trapping movement with the speed of the rolling ball. From this rudimentary beginning, his perception of time-space relationships improves, and he becomes capable of attempting more challenging tasks. As he rises from the sitting position, he learns to chase, stop, and control a rolling or a bouncing ball. The change from the stationary sitting position to more active involvement is an important step in the progression leading to comprehensive catching skill.

The transition from the stage of chasing the ball to the stage of responding to an aerial ball with actual catching movements is neither smooth nor is it rapid. When the child is introduced to this new form of catching, his initial response is rigid and somewhat reminiscent of the delayed reaction of the trapping technique he used to capture a rolling ball while he was sitting. If the aerial ball is presented too early, there is no effective catching response. For example, if a light ball were tossed chest high at a 2-year-old, he probably would make no response, even though his arms were extended prior to the toss. Typically he would let the ball bump against his chest and would chase it after it had dropped to the floor. Before the age of 3 years, the child often needs to be told how to position his arms effectively in readiness for receiving an aerial ball. The child's first active catching response is an event that marks the beginning of a series of common developmental stages leading to mature form for catching an aerial ball.

Deach observed a first stage in catching characterized by a negative reaction and fear of the ball.[2] What appears to be a fear response, can be detected in the form demonstrated by the 4-year-old children in Figure 6–1. There are companion reactions in their form that could be attributed to apprehension. One of these is the turning of the head to the side to avert the eyes and head from the line of the ball, and the other is the slight backward bending of the trunk away from the oncoming ball. Closing the eyes is an equally common indication of apprehension. Seefeldt found no evidence of the fear reaction in his subjects at ages 1½ to 3 years, but saw it in some who were 4, 5, and 6 years of age.[8] His explanation that fear of an aerial ball is behavior conditioned by unsuccessful catching attempts rather than a natural phenomenon seems plausible. But whatever the reason, the fear response is commonplace in the catching behavior of children, and it is found often in their striking as well. Hellweg reported that 6- to 7-year-old unsuccessful catchers as a group closed their eyes prior to contact,[5] and Harper and Struna observed similar behavior in striking.[4]

In anticipation of catching a large light ball, the young catcher stands facing the tosser and provides a scoop for the ball with his

FIG. 6–1. Unsuccessful attempts to catch a large ball by 4-year-old children. Each shows apprehension by turning the head to the side and by leaning backward slightly. The girl's catching effort involves limited movement, and the coordination of the boy's arm action is amiss. His arm action, which is quite common, frequently causes the hands to strike the ball and knock it upward.

extended arms and the front of his trunk. This is little more than preparation for a form of trapping in the upright position. The ball is tossed gently and accurately into the waiting receptacle from a very close distance (Fig. 6–2), and at this point little or no response is required or received from the child. With additional experience, he participates increasingly by spreading his arms in readiness, by grasping at the ball with a clapping motion, and by clutching it against his body to complete the catch (Fig. 6–3). Gradually the front of his body is eliminated from use in

FIG. 6–2. A 33-month-old boy extends his arms before the ball is tossed. He waits for the ball without moving, responds after the ball has touched his hands, and then he gently traps it against his chest. It is essentially a robotlike performance.

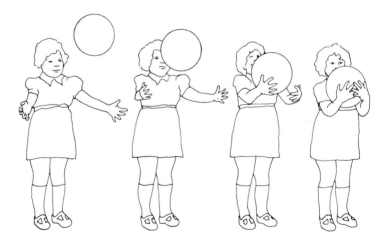

FIG. 6–3. A 4-year-old girl waits for the ball with arms straight and hands spread. Her initial response to the ball is a clapping motion. When one hand contacts the ball, she grasps at it and gains control by clutching it against her chest.

catching, and the ball is cradled in his arms. As he progresses through the developmental phases toward mature form, he brings his hands into play to a greater extent and becomes less dependent upon his arms and body, although he might use his body to help secure the ball. Finally the mature technique is achieved in which the ball is caught using the hands exclusively (Fig. 6–4). Development toward the mature form is encouraged by the use of balls of an increasingly smaller size.

FIG. 6–4. The form used by a 5-year-old boy to make an effective hand catch of a ball thrown softly from a short distance.

During the transition to the form where only the hands are used, development is marked by characteristic changes in arm position. The ball is addressed with the arms straight and forward at shoulder level, then with the arms bent slightly and held lower in front of the body, and finally with the arms lower and forward and the semiflexed elbows pointing distinctly downward. The final position seems to be achieved earlier if the child practices with a small ball rather than mostly with a large one. Apparently the child thinks of using only his hands when catching a small ball. No one thus far has reported a sequence of catching behavior based upon longitudinal data in which children are exposed exclusively to balls of a small size. It is quite possible that the sequence and rate of skill development would be profoundly affected if only a small ball were used.

Arm and hand positions prior to and immediately following contact were analyzed in a cinematic study by Victors.[13] She subjectively evaluated the catching behavior of large groups of 7- and 9-year-old boys, and selected 5 good and 5 poor performers at each age level. Her subjects were filmed while attempting to catch balls 3 inches and 10 inches in diameter, tossed from a distance of 20 feet, and aimed at chest level. The performances of the boys varied considerably and individual catching behavior lacked consistency. It was apparent from the result of the study that the components of catching could be combined successfully in a variety of ways. Several initial arm-hand positions were

FIG. 6–5. Immature arm position used by a 4½-year-old girl. Her arms are straight and too high, and her hands are poorly positioned for simultaneous contact. The catching action in the sequence is premature and unsuccessful.

effective. The only notably unsuccessful initial position was with the arms straight at the elbows and the hands waist high or higher (Fig. 6–5). This position is typical of the immature catching pattern and was used in the study only by unsuccessful 7-year-olds.

Victors also studied the grasping patterns used in the act of catching and found that successful catchers contact the ball simultaneously with both hands and effect closure in the same manner.[13] Hand position varied among successful catchers, but some patterns were used more frequently than others. The one most frequently used was a fingers-forward and palms-up pattern (Fig. 6–1). A viselike position formed by a bottom hand with the palm up and the fingers pointing forward and a top hand with the palm forward and the fingers pointing upward (Fig. 6–6) was also used often and successfully. It is interesting to note the discrepancy between the form used by the children in this study and the form suggested by most textbooks for handling a ball arriving at chest height.

The development of skill in catching has been presented in general terms as a trend toward hand catching which reflects the proximal-distal refinement of nervous control. The development can also be expressed in terms of stages.

The development of catching skill was delineated into 5 stages by Seefeldt, Reuschlein, and Vogel at Michigan State University.[9] They suggested the following:

STAGE 1. The child presents his arms directly in front of him, with the elbows extended and the palm facing upward or inward toward the midsagittal plane. As the ball contacts the hands or

FIG. 6–6. The viselike hand position often used by children when catching a small ball.

arms, the elbows are flexed and the arms and hands attempt to secure the ball by holding it against the chest.

STAGE 2. The child prepares to receive the object with the arms in front of the body, the elbows extended or slightly flexed. Upon presentation of the ball the arms begin an encircling motion that culminates by securing the ball against the chest. The receiver initiates the arm action prior to ball-arm contact.

STAGE 3. The child prepares to receive the ball with arms that are slightly flexed and extended forward at the shoulder. Many children also receive the ball with arms that are flexed at the elbow, with the elbow ahead of a frontal plane.

Substage a. The child uses his chest as the first contact point of the ball and attempts to secure the ball by holding it to his chest with the hands and arms.

Substage b. The child attempts to catch the ball with his hands. Upon his failure to hold it securely, he maneuvers it to his chest, where it is controlled by hands and arms.

STAGE 4. The child prepares to receive the ball by flexing the elbows and presenting the arms ahead of the frontal plane. Skillful performers may keep the elbows at the sides and flex the arms simultaneously as they bring them forward to meet the ball. The ball is caught with the hands, without making contact with other body parts.

STAGE 5. The upper segmental action is identical to that for stage 4. In addition, the child is required to change his stationary base in order to receive the ball.

These stages do not appear to be easily distinguishable. Anyone wishing to use them might benefit by concentrating on the initial position as the ball approaches and the final position after the ball is secure.

MATURE PATTERN OF MOVEMENTS IN THE ACT OF CATCHING

Many aspects of a catch are quite specific and are related to particular catching situations. After all movements and techniques peculiar to special forms of catching are stripped away, a bare pattern of arm and hand actions remains. That basic pattern consists of two phases: (1) moving the hands into an effective position for receiving the ball and (2) grasping and controlling the ball. To clarify the description of the catching pattern, it is assumed here that the ball·to be caught is moving directly at the catcher.

The first phase is preparatory but crucial in terms of the effectiveness of the act of catching. The hands are moved forward to a position in line with the expected trajectory of the ball, and the position is reached prior to or no later than the instant of contact. In the second phase of the pattern, the hands perform in unison to contact and control the ball. After initial contact, the hands and arms give way with the ball in the continued direction of its trajectory. The process allows time for successful closure by the hands and distance over which to exert force to stop the ball. These are the essential aspects of all straightforward catching patterns. Each of the two phases can be amplified to further establish its basic identity.

Preparation for Catching

The function of the arms in the preliminary phase is to move the hands into position for the act of catching. To perform this task, the arms are raised in front of the body, moving the elbows forward of the trunk while allowing them to continue pointing in a downward direction. The precise position in which the hands

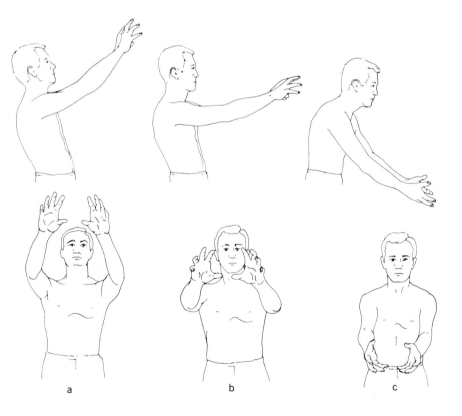

a   b   c

FIG. 6–7. Preparatory hand positions for a ball arriving: (a) above the shoulders, (b) between the waist and shoulders, and (c) below the waist. Fingers point toward the ball and palms face obliquely rather than perpendicularly toward the ball.

must be placed is determined by the trajectory of the ball and its height at the point of contact. If the expected point of contact is almost chest high or above, the hands are raised to that level, the forearms are pronated slightly, and the fingers are pointed forward and upward (Fig. 6–7). The palms face obliquely forward, inward, and downward. If the ball is expected to arrive at waist level or below, the forearms are supinated, positioning the hands with the fingers pointing forward and the palms facing forward, inward, and upward. These two positions automatically juxtapose the thumbs or little fingers in a general way and form a cupped receiving unit with the fingers oriented toward the oncoming ball. Between the waist and lower part of the chest is an awkward area for which neither hand position is fully satisfactory. However, the ball usually is moving in a downward trajectory when it arrives in that area so that the commonly used hand position is with fingers forward and palms up. The flight of the ball finally determines the most effective hand position when the ball arrives slightly above the waist.

A conspicuous feature of the hand position is the manner in which the fingers are extended and point sharply in the direction of the ball immediately before contact. It appears that the fingers are more effective in closure and in controlling the ball when they point forward rather than more directly upward or downward. The illustrations throughout this chapter emphasize the prevalence of the extended finger position.

The Act of Catching

Catching is a force absorption skill. It has been described as the act of reducing the momentum of an object in flight to the point at which it has zero or near zero velocity. This description is used frequently and places heavy emphasis on stopping rather than on controlling the ball. In the act of catching, control is gained by grasping the ball and by stopping its motion. These two requirements are satisfied in a continuous, if not simultaneous, process involving the arms and hands. The catcher contacts the ball with both hands at the same time and instantly begins to grasp and give way with it. Many highly skilled catchers appear to begin the giving way motion just prior to the instant of contact, but this could be another of the illusions of movement. Most of the giving way occurs at the shoulder and elbow joints when the ball is caught in the bare hands. Wrist action is detected in specific catching situations, notably in baseball, but it seems to be a minor movement in the basic catching pattern. The act of catching has been completed when the ball is fully under the catcher's control. If the catcher bobbles the ball during the process of gaining control of it, his performance is successful but less than skillful.

SELECTED MECHANICAL PRINCIPLES APPLICABLE TO CATCHING

Two principles are of vital importance in gaining control of the ball:

1. Force must be applied to change the velocity of a body (to decelerate the ball).
2. The shock of catching can be diminished by absorbing it either over a greater distance or over a greater area, or both (arms must give with the ball).

VARIATIONS INVOLVING THE BASIC PATTERN OF CATCHING

Catching is an important skill in many of the games played in elementary schools. In the simple games played at the primary grade level, a medium-sized playground ball is used, and boys and girls play together. However, there is a tendency to present organized sports to boys at increasingly lower grade levels and to splinter girls off to less demanding games and activities. This practice affords boys the opportunity for early exposure to specialized catching skills involving a variety of balls and unfortunately opens a gap in catching skill between boys and girls that remains unbridged. However, children of both sexes eventually use special catching skills in basketball and softball, and boys add to their repertoire the catching skills in football. These sports require the basic pattern of catching to be used in a way that is determined by the physical characteristics of different types of balls and the specialized uses of the balls in games.

Catching the Basketball Pass

The strong element of keep away in the game of basketball requires careful execution of passing and catching skills. The passer must direct the ball at the receiver briskly and accurately; the catcher often must step toward the oncoming ball and reach out to shorten the distance it travels. Stepping toward the ball is strategically effective, but at the same time it increases the potential force of the ball at contact and complicates the timing of the catching movements. These difficulties are minor and do nothing to mask the presence of the basic pattern, which stands out vividly. In Figure 6–8, the player steps toward the ball, bends his trunk so that his arms can stretch forward, and keeps his elbows bent slightly and pointing downward. The fingers of his hands are well spread and pointing toward the ball

FIG. 6–8. Catching a basketball pass. The player steps toward the ball, partially extends his arms, spreads his fingers, and points them at the ball. Simultaneous contact is followed by giving at the elbow and shoulder joints.

to provide a large contact surface for satisfactory control. There is simultaneous contact and closure by both hands, and the arms give with the ball by bending at the elbows and the shoulders.

Catching the Football

Football is a game offering a wide variety of situations in which the ball must be caught. Ordinarily the player who catches the ball has the immediate secondary responsibility of kicking it or running with it. A basic pattern of catching movements is used, and the details of technique vary to accommodate the total situation.

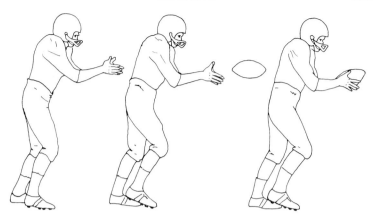

FIG. 6-9. Catching a centered football in preparation for a punt.

CATCHING A CENTERED FOOTBALL. When the ball is centered, it spins around its long axis, travels at a brisk rate of speed, and must be caught in the hands only. The punter in Figure 6-9 steps toward the ball and demonstrates the same basic pattern of catching that was used by the basketball player in Figure 6-8. His arms are extended, his fingers point toward the ball, and his hands are in position for simultaneous contact. The punter necessarily limits the distance he uses for stopping the ball. Immediately after he catches it, he must realign the ball in his hands while moving forward and then drop it in preparation for the kick.

CATCHING A PASSED FOOTBALL. The passed football is difficult to catch because it spins rapidly and moves with substantial velocity. The player assigned to be the receiver may be in a stationary position awaiting the ball and an imminent tackle, he may be running at a right angle to the expected trajectory of the ball, or he may be moving away from the passer and in the same direction as the passed ball. In each instance the designated receiver's primary responsibility is to concentrate on catching the ball. His catching technique, which often includes a degree of "trapping," reflects the circumstances of his immediate position and anticipates the secondary tasks of protecting the ball and running with it.

The player in Figure 6-10a is in position and waiting for the ball to arrive. Since the ball will be in a downward flight when it is caught, his fingers are well spread and pointing forward, and his palms face upward. As the ball is received, it will be grasped and brought to a secure position trapped against the front of his

FIG. 6–10. Catching a football pass: (a) from a stationary position, (b) while running at a diagonal to the thrown ball, (c) while running perpendicular to the flight of the ball, and (d) while running in the same direction as the flight of the ball.

trunk. The ball will be held in that snug position until the receiver can turn and reorient himself from the task of catching to the job of running.

If the catcher runs a path that is perpendicular or oblique to the flight of the ball (Figs. 6–10b, c), he adjusts the length of his arms so his hands can make simultaneous contact. He frequently allows the ball to touch his trunk or chest while stopping and controlling it during the catch. Later the ball is moved to a position that is secure and yet does not interfere with effective arm movement while running.

A player who runs in the same direction as the flight of the ball may have to reach back to catch it or may have to catch the ball over his shoulder. In either case the catcher benefits from the fact that the relative velocity of the ball at contact has been reduced by an amount equal to his running speed. Effective eye-hand coordination is a more significant problem than stopping the ball in this variation of catching. During the time the receiver is preparing to catch the ball, his eyes are between his hands and the ball. This is a reversal of the normal relationship and is the source of difficult eye-hand coordination. The receiver must raise his arms, position his hands for simultaneous contact, and adjust for the downward flight of the ball (Fig. 6–10d). Spectacular over-the-shoulder catches are made occasionally in which the ball is first contacted with one hand. After the problem of eye-hand coordination is surmounted at initial contact, the ball can be brought under control with a minimum of difficulty because the body and the ball move in the same direction.

Catching with a Gloved Hand

In baseball and softball when a special glove is used to assist in catching, the basic pattern is modified slightly. Simultaneous closure by both hands is neither necessary nor strictly possible. The gloved hand assumes the primary responsibility for stopping and controlling the ball. In Figure 6–11, the ball is moving directly at the pocket of the glove, and the fingers of the bare hand point toward the ball in readiness to close over it after it has struck the glove. The bare hand helps control the ball after contact, but more importantly, it grasps the ball from the pocket of the glove in preparation for a quick throw.

The size of the baseball glove and its special properties for stopping and controlling the ball give an enormous boost to the catching skill of young boys. If a 7- or 8-year-old boy can position his glove in the path of the moving ball, he has a reasonable chance of making a successful catch because the large padded

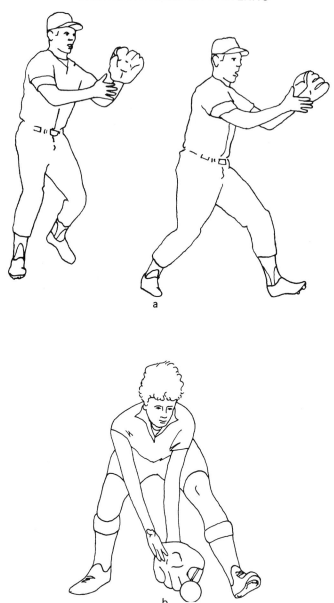

FIG. 6–11. Catching with a gloved hand. (a) The player anticipates the need to throw quickly and steps toward the ball. His gloved hand is positioned to stop the ball, and his bare hand is ready to cover and grasp it. (b) The player positions her gloved hand to stop the ball. Her bare hand is ready to help control the ball and grasp it for a fast throw.

glove tends to envelop the ball when contact is made. Encouraged by early success in catching with a glove, the boy tends to develop a one-handed catching technique. The glove gives him a relatively wide margin for error, and he confidently puts it in the path of the ball with high hope and little concern for the lack of cooperation from his bare hand.

Wrist action gains importance when the glove is used in catching. A ball caught with the glove is contacted farther away from the wrist and higher on the hand than when using a bare-handed form. The large pocket encases the ball at contact, and wrist extension becomes a more important movement in the giving action used to stop the ball. The tethered pocket of the glove minimizes the danger of the ball rolling backward off the fingers when the wrist gives in the act of catching.

Aside from the departure in the action of the hands caused by the use of the glove, the basic pattern of catching is used in baseball and in softball. The player reaches out for the ball with elbows remaining bent and pointing downward, the hand is positioned to stop and grasp the ball, and the force of the ball is diminished by use of the glove and a giving action by the wrist, elbow, and shoulder.

FIG. 6–12.   A 7-year-old boy moving to make a successful catch of a large ball.

ANALYSIS OF FORM IN CATCHING

The act of catching is not performed so quickly that many of its features are lost to direct visual observation as is the case with several other fundamental skills. Simultaneous contact and closure are the most difficult aspects of the pattern to perceive. With this in mind, other phases of the pattern can be concentrated upon in direct analysis of catching. The analyzer might direct his attention primarily to the preparatory and the final actions. He could check for:

1. Promptness and accuracy of precatch movement to a position in line with the trajectory of the ball.
2. An outreaching arm position with elbows bent somewhat and pointing downward.
3. Hands being in position to intercept the ball in its trajectory prior to contact.
4. Hand(s) contact only.
5. Giving with arms at shoulder and elbow to absorb the force of the ball.

The degree to which the above simple criteria are met will be a broad indication of progress toward or the existence of mature form. The sequences in Figures 6–1, 6–2, 6–3, 6–4, 6–5, 6–12, 6–13, and 6–14 offer an opportunity to use the suggested checks. The same figures can be examined for the presence of the characteristics in each of the five stages identified by Seefeldt, Reuschlein, and Vogel.[9] This combined practice should provide a solid basis for actual direct analysis later.

FIG. 6–13.   An 8-year-old boy moves forward to catch the ball.

FIG. 6–14. A successful catch of a small ball by a 7-year-old boy.

BIBLIOGRAPHY

1. Bruce, R.: The Effects of Variations in Ball Trajectory Upon the Catching Performance of Elementary School Children. Unpublished Doctoral Dissertation, University of Wisconsin, 1966.
2. Deach, D.: Genetic Development of Motor Skills in Children Two Through Six Years of Age. Unpublished Doctoral Dissertation, University of Michigan, 1950.
3. Gutteridge, M.: A Study of motor achievements of young children. Arch. Psychol., No. 244, New York, 1939.
4. Harper, C. J., and Struna, N. L.: Case Studies in the Development of One-Handed Striking. Research Paper, AAHPER Meeting, Minneapolis, 1973.
5. Hellweg, D. A.: An Analysis of Perceptual and Performance Characteristics of the Catching Skill in 6–7-Year-Old Children. Unpublished Doctoral Dissertation, University of Wisconsin, 1972.
6. Hoadley, D.: A Study of the Catching Ability of Children in Grades One to Four. Unpublished Master's Thesis, University of Iowa, 1941.
7. Pederson, E. J.: A Study of Ball Catching Abilities of First-, Third-, and Fifth-Grade Children on Twelve Selected Ball Catching Tasks. Unpublished Doctoral Dissertation, Indiana University, 1973.
8. Seefeldt, V.: Developmental Sequence of Catching Skill. Paper presented at AAHPER Meeting, Houston, 1972.
9. Seefeldt, V., Reuschlein, S., and Vogel, P.: Sequencing Motor Skills Within the Physical Education Curriculum. Paper presented at AAHPER Meeting, Houston, 1972.
10. Seils, L.: The relationship between measures of physical growth and gross motor performance of primary grade children. Res. Q. Am. Assoc. Health Phys. Educ., 22:244, 1951.
11. Sinclair, C.: Movement and Movement Patterns of Early Childhood. Division of Educational Research and Statistics, State Dept. of Education, Richmond, Va., 1971.
12. Torres, J. A.: Relationship Between Figure-Ground Perceptual Ability and Ball Catching Ability in 10- and 13-Year-Old Boys and Girls. Research Paper, AAHPER Meeting, St. Louis, 1968.

13. Victors, E.: A Cinematical Analysis of Catching Behavior of a Selected Group of 7- and 9-Year-Old Boys. Unpublished Doctoral Dissertation, University of Wisconsin, 1961.
14. Warner, A. P.: The Motor Ability of Third, Fourth, and Fifth Grade Boys in the Elementary School. Unpublished Doctoral Dissertation, University of Michigan, 1952.
15. Whiting, H. T. A.: Acquiring Ball Skill. London, G. Bell and Sons, Ltd., 1969.
16. Whiting, H. T. A., Gill, E. B., and Stephenson, J. M.: Critical time intervals for taking in-flight information in a ball catching task. Ergonomics, *13*:(2), 265, 1970.
17. Williams, H.: The Effects of Systematic Variation of Speed and Direction of Object Flight and of Skill and Age Classifications Upon Visuo-perceptual Judgments of Moving Objects in Three-Dimensional Space. Unpublished Doctoral Dissertation, University of Wisconsin, 1968.

7

STRIKING

Striking skills are a conglomerate of movements occurring in a variety of planes and under varying circumstances. Overarm, sidearm, and underhand patterns are common with a variety of implements being used for striking in each pattern. Among the implements used are body parts including the hand, the head, and the foot and special pieces of equipment such as the bat, the racket, the paddle, and the club. Kicking is one of the major types of striking, but because of its relative importance as a basic skill it has been selected for separate, detailed treatment in the following chapter. Of the striking skills remaining after the isolation of kicking, the skills most commonly used are those that are performed in a sidearm pattern. Therefore, the development of striking in the sidearm pattern will receive major emphasis in this chapter, with minor attention being given to patterns performed in other planes.

PERFORMANCES OF CHILDREN IN STRIKING SKILLS

Information concerning the performances of children using striking skills is precious, indeed. The dearth of information appears to be related directly to the slow rate at which measurable skill develops. The young child frequently can swing a bat or a paddle with reasonably effective form before he is able to hit an object in such a way that he can obtain a quantitative score for his performance. Obviously, swinging and striking are not the same. Evaluation of the form used for striking is a useful indication of the quality of the movement pattern, but it does not reveal anything specific about the ability to strike an object. Currently there does not appear to be an effective way to measure striking performance objectively at the preschool level.

Efforts to use standard measures of performance in striking

have been confined largely to the testing of school age children. Even at this level, the results provide little more than a sketchy picture of the ability of children to use striking skills. Seils studied the motor performances of 510 primary grade children ranging in age from 71 to 106 months.[15] In his battery of gross motor performance tests, striking was measured by the use of a pendulum-controlled ball that was to be struck by a bat. The average performances on the test showed a constant increase for both boys and girls at successive grade levels. However, when all of the children were classified according to 3-month age intervals rather than grade, there was no evidence of constant improvement. Johnson used a procedure for testing striking skill which was similar to the one used by Seils.[11] The 624 elementary school children in grades 1 through 6 who were tested were asked to strike a ball that was swung over the plate. The average scores on the batting test were increasingly better at successive grade levels. Boys were considerably better performers on the batting test at grades 1 and 2, but thereafter retained only a slight advantage over the girls.

Sheehan provided some information relative to a broad trend in the batting performance of boys at the elementary school level.[16] One group in his study corresponded to the primary grade level (ages 7, 8, and 9), and another to the intermediate grade level (ages 10, 11, and 12). The boys batted in a situation that was realistic but not completely controlled. Each was given 10 hits during a baseball batting practice in which the ball was thrown the regulation pitching distance by another player. The respective average scores of 21.6 and 27.1 for the two groups, suggest an improvement in batting ability for boys of elementary school age.

The volleyball serve for distance was used to measure striking performance in an underarm pattern using the hand as the striking implement. According to the scores registered by the 2840 elementary school children tested by Hanson, boys and girls improve regularly in this form of striking.[9] The average distance the volleyball was served was significantly greater at successive grade levels, and boys served farther than girls in each grade.

The paucity of evidence concerning the performance of children using striking skills is a signal for caution. There are suggestions of a general trend toward regular improvement during the elementary school period, but the rate and the nature of the improvement are quite vague and need to be studied much more extensively.

DEVELOPMENTAL FORM IN STRIKING

The earliest form used in striking seems to be derived from an overarm motion that occurs in the anteroposterior plane. The child naturally uses this action whenever he hits something with his hand, and he makes little effort to modify his movement if given an implement with which to strike (Fig. 7-1). The simplicity of the pattern is consistent with the abilities of the young child whose reaction time, movement time, strength, balance, and perception are limited. When he uses the overarm pattern, he can face the object to be struck and gain the advantage of being able to look directly at it throughout the striking movement. The pattern permits him to limit the total range of motion and the number of levers to be applied while striking, thereby reducing the amount of strength, balance, total time, and coordination required. The overarm pattern offers him the largest assurance of success in most tasks involving striking, and he continually reverts to it when he needs a high probability for success.[8] There is a constant threat of intrusion by the overarm striking pattern when the child tries to learn to strike in the horizontal plane. He finds it difficult to abandon the natural but ineffective overarm motion for the more complicated but useful sidearm pattern. The deep-rooted nature of the immature overarm swing is evidenced by the manner in which it lingers and reappears for many years in a variety of sport skills.

The emergence and progression of the overarm striking pattern was observed coincidentally by Deach in connection with her investigation of the development of striking skill in the underhand pattern.[4] Her 2- to 6-year-old subjects were given the task of using an underhand volleyball serving motion to strike a ball held in the opposite hand. The ball was first given impetus by an overarm throwing motion without any indication of a hit. This initial technique was superseded by a push and by an overhand hit before the underhand striking pattern was achieved. Halverson and Roberton observed the same overhand pattern when children were first asked to hit a ball from their own toss.[7] During the phases in which the overarm pattern was used by Deach's subjects, there were accompanying changes in the movements of the legs. From a stationary position, progress was made to a forward step with a same arm-leg pattern, and was followed by the mature opposite arm-leg pattern. Corresponding enlargement of the rotatory movements of the hips and trunk accompanied the changes in the leg pattern. In general, the early phases in the development of the underhand striking pattern seemed to unfold in a sequence quite similar to the early developmental sequence for the skill of throwing. However, this observation should not be interpreted to mean that the overhand throwing motion emerges before the overhand striking motion. Since infants seem to strike as well as they throw when using the overarm pattern, perhaps it is erroneous to assume that the

throwing motion generally occurs prior to and is the basis for the typical pounding or striking movement.

Sidearm Pattern

If the child is allowed to develop his striking skills without special assistance, he seems to progress slowly from striking in a vertical plane (Fig. 7–2), downward through a series of increasingly flatter oblique planes to an effective pattern predominantly in a horizontal plane (Fig. 7–3; 7–4). He tends to progress to the pattern in the latter plane earlier if provided encouraging opportunities to practice those common striking skills in the sidearm pattern which are basically task oriented and sport skill related.

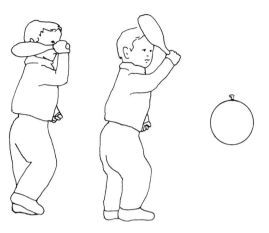

FIG. 7–1. Immature overarm striking pattern. The striking action by the 22-month-old child is primarily an extension of his forearm. After preliminary steps and a brief pause, he steps forward using a unitary same arm–same leg pattern and confines his movements to the anteroposterior plane.

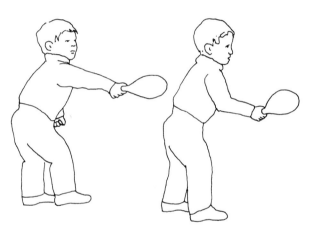

The development of form in the sidearm striking pattern has been one of the concerns in an open-ended longitudinal study that began at the University of Wisconsin in 1962. A preliminary report in 1966 indicated that Halverson and Roberton were able to manipulate the circumstances in their film studies of young children and elicit a reasonably natural striking movement in the sidearm pattern.[7] They supplied the children with equipment that was manageable in terms of weight and length, suspended a ball or tossed one to them at waist level, and encouraged them to strike with increasing force, hitting toward a particular person. Only a few children were involved, but their responses were filmed and refilmed at regular intervals, thus enabling the investigators to observe developmental changes in the striking

patterns. In the early attempts to strike in the sidearm pattern, arm action initiated the movement and was followed by limited spinal and pelvic rotation. The pelvis and trunk rotated as a unit, and the block rotation appeared to be a result of the swing rather than a contributing force. Progressively the children abandoned the arm-dominated pattern and replaced it with one in which there was a forward weight shift, a greater range of joint actions, and more separation of the rotatory elements in the striking pattern. As the difficulty of the tasks presented to the children was increased, the number of successes decreased and there was deterioration of the pattern and retrogression to less mature form. This study is particularly important because Halverson and her associates have continued to observe the same children and to collect data concerning individual progress in the

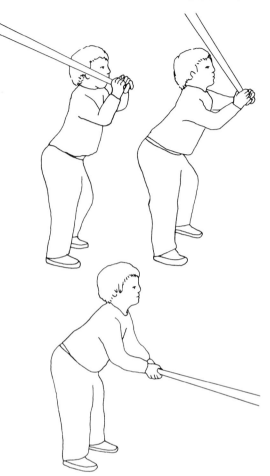

FIG. 7–2. Swing in a vertical plane. The child (age 33 months) turns to face the object squarely and then swings the bat, extending her forearms and uncocking her wrists. Her forward trunk bend is the counterpart of rotation that develops around a vertical axis in more mature form.

development of striking skills. Periodic reports of their observations include information regarding the factors that affect performance in striking and the individual responses of children to each of those factors.

A report on the development of one-handed striking in two children from Halverson's longitudinal study detailed changes observed in the patterns used by a 3-year-old boy and a 3-year-old girl who had been filmed several times over a period of a year.[10] The girl began with an arm-dominated pattern and no weight shift or trunk rotation. She progressed during the year to a swing initiated by a forward step and followed by simultaneous block rotation and arm swing. Since the boy had demonstrated this pattern on all four trials, his progress was noted primarily in terms of subtle changes, including an increase in the length of

FIG. 7–3. A 4-year-old boy attempts to strike a ball using a sidearm pattern. His swing in the upper series is "top-dominated" and rigidly performed. Immediately after the unsuccessful swing, he drew back the bat and reswung. The swing in the lower series obviously is more forceful, and the form is improved in nearly every respect.

FIG. 7–4. A 4-year-old child demonstrates the general movement pattern used in an effective swing in a horizontal plane. He rotates around his long axis and lowers his bat to meet the downward arching trajectory of the ball. There is clear evidence of "opening" in the pattern.

the initial stride. The investigators suggested that "opening" appears in the sidearm striking pattern as soon as the child begins to use a forward step to initiate his swing.

Thirty-three children between the ages of 21 and 60 months were filmed while attempting to perform striking movements in a sidearm pattern with a bat and with a paddle under various conditions.[19] These preschool children used striking patterns similar to the ones observed by Halverson, with the exception that those who were less than 30 months old invariably used the overarm pattern when striking at a suspended object with either of the implements. They adjusted to the height of the ball by bending forward at the waist before starting to strike. The amount of forward trunk bend was increased as the height of the ball was lowered. Some turned to face the ball in a preliminary adjustment, and others occasionally accompanied the turn with a forward step by the leg on the same side as the striking motion. Although the overarm pattern tended to persist, children beyond the age of 30 months responded favorably when encouraged to strike a suspended ball using a one- or a two-arm pattern in a horizontal plane. Progress in the development of an effective striking pattern was indicated by the changes observed in the patterns used at successive ages. Some of these changes were:

1. More freedom in the swing with increased range of motion at the various joints (unfreezing of the unitary rotatory motion).
2. More use of the forward step or a forward weight shift to initiate the pattern (delaying arm action, causing "opening").
3. More definite hip and trunk rotation preceding the action of the arms in the swing.
4. More distinct uncocking of the wrists during the swing.

When using a two-arm swing, several of the 4-year-old children demonstrated a pattern of striking that was amazingly similar to the mature pattern (Fig. 7–4). They initiated the movement with a forward weight shift, then rotated their hips and trunks, and followed smoothly with an arm swing, uncocking their wrists just prior to contact.

Most of the children seemed to be slightly more effective with the two-arm than with the one-arm swing. Perhaps part of the reason for the advantage was that batting practice was available in the nursery school activities program for anyone who was interested. Another factor was the apparent presence of the concept that one does not swing a paddle as vigorously as he swings a bat. Effective patterns in either version were demonstrated *only* when the child used a full and forceful swing. The forceful swing increased his range of motion and helped differentiate the movements in the pattern. Even when younger children used rather wild striking motions, the swings were consistently *more mature in form* although not necessarily more successful in terms of actual hitting.

Oblique Pattern

Heretofore the literature contained no report of the striking behavior of children when they were striking downward in an oblique plane. The subjects in the Wickstrom study were also given an opportunity to use what would be the broad equivalent of the golf swing. A ball was placed on the mat in front of the child; he was handed a bat and asked if he could hit the ball in a particular predetermined direction. The responses to the task were diverse but contained enough common elements to suggest wide developmental directions. The youngest children used an overarm chopping movement exclusively, striking the top of the ball in the process (Fig. 7–5). They bent at the knees and waist to start the movement and immediately followed with a downward arm-dominated swing. This swing was merely an extension of the type of overarm pattern that was used to strike a ball suspended at waist height. The older children in this sub-5-year-old group showed progress into two additional roughly structured stages. In the first of these, the child moved his bat out to the side, bent at the knees or waist to lower his trunk, and used a sidearm batting swing (Fig. 7–6). Frequently a forward step initiated the sequence and emphasized the chop-push character of the swing. The more advanced stage was characterized by an initial weight shift accompanied by a sideward and downward bat swing and a slight forward bend of the trunk. It was followed by and concluded with uncocking of the wrists and unitary rotation in the follow-through (Fig. 7–7). The latter stage produced a swing predominantly in a single oblique plane, but it, as well as the previous stage, lacked early rotation of the pelvis and trunk and was an arm-dominated movement pattern.

Responses to the task of hitting a ball on the ground indicated that a few of the children already possessed some of the rudiments of a golf swing. It is quite possible that preschool children are ready for work with advanced striking skills requiring limited perceptual judgments at a much earlier age than is currently expected. Further study of striking tasks of this sort will be needed before an evaluation of the above findings can be undertaken and realistic expectations set for skill development. The tentative findings should lead to optimism.

FIG. 7–5. Typical use of the immature overhand striking pattern in an attempt to strike a ball that is on the ground. In the lower sequence, the 33-month-old child bent at the knees and waist as she performed the chopping swing. The 49-month-old girl in the upper series released a hand and used the bat as a hammer.

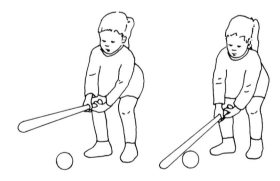

FIG. 7–6. Beginning of a golf-type swing in an oblique plane. A step is taken, and the bat is swung downward and then pushed forward in a sidearm pattern. The 4-year-old boy lowers his body early in the swing so the sidearm batting motion can be executed from a more favorable position.

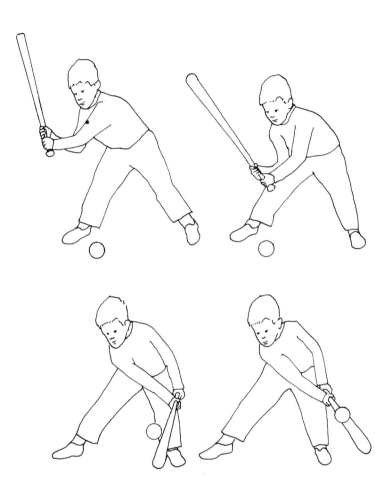

FIG. 7–7. Golf-swing pattern of a 4-year-old girl showing an improvement over the form used in Figure 7–6. The bat starts sideward and downward, accompanied by weight shift and little if any rotation. Wrists uncock and the follow-through keeps the bat primarily in one plane of movement. Typically, the form for the striking task is more effective than the performance.

THE MATURE PATTERN USED IN STRIKING

The mature pattern for all the common striking skills contains a basic sequence consisting of three swiftly merging movements. The sequence can be described briefly as Step–Turn–Swing.

1. Body weight is shifted in the direction of the intended hit while shoulders and arms are coiled in the opposite direction.
2. Hips and spine are rotated in rapid succession in the same direction as the weight shift.
3. Arm(s) swing around and forward in close succession with the other rotatory movements.

Each type of striking skill has its own body of detailed movements that fit around the basic three-point pattern. The timing of the movements is task specific and is a critical distinguishing factor in each sport skill.

SELECTED MECHANICAL PRINCIPLES USED IN STRIKING

In the step-turn-swing pattern used in striking, the timing of the movements and the effective development of velocity are explained by several familiar mechanical principles.

1. Additional linear and angular velocity may be gained by increasing the distance over which force is applied (cocking of the joints on the backswing).
2. Linear and angular movements must be integrated without loss of the benefits of either (step-turn combination).
3. When several forces are applied in succession, each succeeding force must be applied at the point where the preceding one has made its greatest contribution in imparting velocity (the uncocking of joints in the rotatory sequence).
4. Greater linear velocity is possible by increasing the length of the lever used (extension of the arms and uncocking of the wrists).

The extent to which some of these principles are applicable is determined by the value of linear velocity to the outcome of the skill pattern. The importance of speed and accuracy to the striking skills used in games will be evident later.

SPORT SKILLS USING THE BASIC PATTERN FOR STRIKING

Baseball Batting

There are many variables in successful hitting in baseball, including judgments, adjustments, and the swing. The swing is probably the most stable of all the factors. In the swing, the batter attempts to develop as much velocity with his bat as he can without sacrificing his control over its movement. The design of the basic pattern of his swing helps him produce the desired bat velocity.

In the course of the baseball swing, the body rotates approximately 90 degrees, and the bat moves through an arc of 180 degrees before contact (Fig. 7-8). When the forces producing these movements are applied correctly, there is a continuous acceleration of the bat that causes velocity to increase until contact is made with the ball.[14] The batter cocks himself for the swing by assuming a position in which his side is turned toward the pitcher, his weight is toward his back foot, and his bat is cocked around his back shoulder (Fig. 7-9). The swing consists of a step in the direction of the ball, a forward rotation of the hips and spine, and the uncocking of the arms and wrists. In essence, this is the mature pattern for all striking skills.

The precise timing for the addition of each new force in the pattern is determined by individual abilities. Kitzman found that all the batters in his electromyographic study used the same

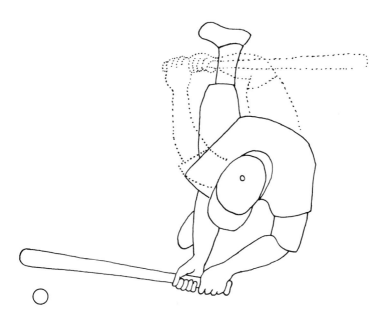

FIG. 7-8. Range of motion of the swing in baseball batting. The bat swings around as well as forward due to the forward step of batter. He rotates his trunk approximately 90 degrees and swings his bat through an elongated arc of about 180 degrees before the bat contacts the ball.

FIG. 7-9. Mature pattern of batting form. The sequence starts with the forward step, followed quickly by hip, trunk, and arm rotation. Forward movement of the trunk stops before contact, but a whipping rotation from the shoulders and arms continues. The pushing motion of the right arm and an uncocking of the wrists at impact are the final significant forces that produce bat velocity.

basic movement pattern, but the experienced batters had earlier involvement of primary muscles, a fact implying an earlier application of certain forces.[12] Another factor in the timing of the movements is the cessation of forward movement onto the front leg. The forward leg acts to stabilize the trunk for final rotatory movements in the latter phase of the pattern (Fig. 7-9) and contributes to the link action or whipping motion of the swing. The batter actually blocks further forward movement with a locked, almost straight front leg before the bat is swung fully around for contact. Children quickly develop this refinement after they learn to use the forward shift of weight to initiate the striking motion (Fig. 7-4).

The final speed of the bat is determined, in part, by the length of the batter's forward arm during the swing. To produce a longer lever for greater bat velocity, the forward arm becomes nearly straight at the elbow early in the arm swing. The front arm stabilizes at an angle of 168 to 177 degrees at the elbow,[5] but the forearm of the back arm continues to extend vigorously to couple with the forward arm for a significant contribution to the so-called final wrist snap at contact. Many details of the swing in baseball batting, including the timing of the parts of the basic pattern, combine to satisfy the specific objective of high bat velocity at impact.

Forehand Stroke in Tennis

In the game of tennis the player frequently must scurry about on the court and hurriedly adapt his strokes merely to keep the ball in play. Under these circumstances he tries to be as effective as possible and attempts to retain most of the elements of his basic stroke pattern. He invariably applies the basic step-turn-swing pattern with appropriate specifics when he has ample time for the execution of a full stroke.

The player pivots smoothly into position ready for his swing in the standard ground stroke. He shifts his weight to his back foot, rotates his body 45 to 90 degrees from the net, cocking his hips and trunk, and draws his racket arm back away from the net. Then in an almost simultaneous succession of movements, he shifts his weight toward the net and continues with forward

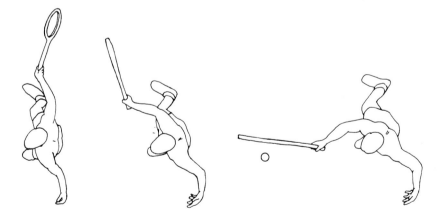

FIG. 7-10. Top view of the forehand stroke in tennis. The weight shifts forward, the hips and trunk rotate, and the arm swings the racket forward in an elongated arc. (Drawn from film loaned by Jean Blievernicht.)

rotation of his hips, trunk, and racket arm.[6] During the forward swing his racket arm remains relatively straight at the elbow and uncocks slightly at the wrist (Fig. 7-10).

Accuracy takes precedence over sheer velocity as a point of emphasis in tennis ground strokes. In a study of the factors involved in the accuracy of the forehand stroke, Blievernicht concluded that skilled players do not change any particular part of the basic swing to control direction.[1] They simply adjust all segments from the beginning of the stroke to achieve the desired racket position at contact. The problem of accuracy is not so easily solved by beginning players. They usually neglect to step forward and tend to overemphasize rotation, thus failing to achieve the elongated arc that moves the racket forward and contributes to accuracy. Beginners tend to revert to the overhand pushing motion characteristic of the immature striking pattern if they are unsuccessful in controlling the lateral direction of the ball. Unfortunately it is possible to get a temporary improvement in accuracy with the immature stroke, but it is not possible to make progress in achieving an effective pattern of striking. Given the advantage of appropriate practice, young children can develop a creditable tennis swing without the necessity of being mired in the pushing stage (Fig. 7-11).

Golf Stroke

Striking is performed under unique circumstances in the game of golf. A stationary ball is struck by a player who has an

FIG. 7-11. A forehand stroke by a 6-year-old boy. He shows preparatory cocking of his body, forward shift of weight, rotation of hips and spine, and sidearm swing. (Courtesy of World Tennis.)

FIG. 7–12. Mature golf swing. Club head develops velocity through approximately a 270-degree arc prior to impact. The basic shift-turn-swing pattern for striking skills appears in close sequence in this particular sport skill.

unhurried opportunity to adjust his position and prepare for the swing. The seeming advantage of hitting a nonmoving ball does not significantly reduce the inherent difficulty of the task. The golfer's complex problem is to coordinate all the movements in his swing so that the head at the end of the golf club is moving with high velocity and is precisely positioned at impact. He has virtually no margin for error.

The golf stroke is a complicated striking skill, and yet the basic pattern of movements is plainly applicable. The joints are cocked by rotating the hips and trunk away from the ball, bringing the club up and around to a position behind the back shoulder, and cocking the wrists (Fig. 7–12). Acceleration of the club head on the downswing is extremely rapid with the forces producing it being applied in lightning succession. The downward swing is completed in a fraction of a second. The sequence is the familiar shift of body weight toward the forward foot, forward rotation of the hips and spine, downward swing of the forward arm, and uncocking of the back arm and wrists (Fig. 7–12). In the downswing the club head moves in a single plane and describes a long forward arc caused by the shift of body weight. Carlsöö's preliminary comparison of the golf swings of championship and average players revealed an arm-dominated pattern in the latter group.[2] He suggested that average players do not use the momentum of the trunk, swing mostly with the arms, and often fail to apply wrist movement at the end of the downswing. In children, these features would be associated with developmental patterns.

Underhand Volleyball Serve

The underhand serve in volleyball is used by a comparatively small number of competitive players because other serves have greater offensive value. This particular serve is included here because it is a familiar sport skill, and it illustrates striking in an underhand pattern. The pattern combines forward and rotatory movements to produce a controlled hit with submaximal velocity. Rotation in the underhand pattern is predominantly around a horizontal axis in contrast to rotation in the sidearm pattern which is mostly around a vertical axis. Figure 7–13 shows that the server's arm moves forward in basically the same plane and that rotation around his long axis is confined to the upper spine and shoulders. The server steps forward while cocking his arm backward and upward, he rotates his shoulders to the left as he

FIG. 7–13. Underhand volleyball serve. The server cocks his arm backward and upward as he steps forward, he rotates his shoulders to the left as the striking arm swings forward, and he drops his support hand away from the ball just before contact. A high floating trajectory is the result.

swings his striking arm forward, and he drops his support hand from under the ball just before contact. The high trajectory of the ball is consistent with the type of serve.

ANALYSIS OF FORM IN STRIKING

The specific striking skills used in sports are difficult for the child to learn. Most children perform the skills with glee but with very limited measurable success. Their early success is noted more in terms of improvement in movement pattern than in terms of actual hitting. Because of this circumstance, analysis of form becomes the solitary practical means of assessing the striking behavior of young children.

The basic trend in striking from overhand to sidearm patterns with typical developmental characteristics should be reviewed before gross analysis of striking is attempted. Because motor patterns change according to the velocity of the swing, swings of the same type ought to be grouped for analysis, starting with the high-velocity type. It is difficult to detect the sequence of rotation in the trunk and the action of the wrists in high-velocity swings, but many important features can be observed directly. When observing a vigorous striking motion in the horizontal plane, the following items may be employed to help determine the relative maturity of the form used:

1. In preparation for the swing, the body is rotated away from the object to be struck.
2. There is a forward stride with accompanying weight shift.
3. The striking implement is cocked further as the stride begins.
4. There is a blocking action of the forward leg after the stride.
5. The trunk is rotated forcefully.
6. The implement is whipped around and forward, with the dominant arm remaining relatively straight.
7. The swing is basically in the horizontal plane (not an oblique chopping motion).

Obviously it is necessary to observe several swings in order to check carefully for the presence of the features noted above. It usually helps greatly to look first for evidence of "opening" in the swing, and then continue to search for other pattern elements. The sequences in Figures 7–1, 7–2, 7–3, 7–4, 7–5, 7–6, 7–7, 7–9, (mature form), 7–14, 7–15, and 7–16 can be used to practice the analysis of striking skills. The ability to pick out top-dominated, unitary, and sequential patterns quickly, however, will be acquired only with practice involving actual swings in high-velocity striking attempts.

FIG. 7–14. Prior to being filmed, the 4½-year-old girl shown in this figure had never had a bat in her hands. Which aspects of the basic pattern does she use naturally?

FIG. 7–15. A downward striking pattern of a 4½-year-old boy.

FIG. 7–16. Striking patterns of the same boy at age 5 years, 3 months. Upper: one-arm swing. Lower: two-arm swing.

BIBLIOGRAPHY

1. Blievernicht, J.: Accuracy in the tennis forehand drive: Cinematographic analysis. Res. Q. Am. Assoc. Health Phys. Educ., *33*:776, 1968.
2. Carlsöö, S.: Kinematic analysis of the golf swing. *In* Medicine and Sport, Vol. II: Biomechanics (Wartenweiler, Jokl, and Hebbelinck, eds.). Baltimore, University Park Press, 1968.
3. Cooper, J., and Glassow, R.: Kinesiology. St. Louis, C. V. Mosby Co., 1972.
4. Deach, D.: Genetic Development of Motor Skills in Children Two Through Six Years of Age. Unpublished Doctoral Dissertation, University of Michigan, 1950.
5. Finley, R.: Kinesiological Analysis of Human Motion. Unpublished D. P. E. Thesis, Springfield College, 1961.
6. Gelner, J.: Analysis of Some of the Body Levers Contributing to the Force in a Tennis Forehand Drive. Unpublished Cinematographic Analysis, University of Wisconsin, 1963.
7. Halverson, L. E., and Roberton, M. A.: A Study of Motor Pattern Development in Young Children. Report to the National Convention of AAHPER, Chicago, 1966.
8. Halverson, L. E., Roberton, M. A., and Harper, C. J.: Current research in motor development. J. Res. Dev. Educ., *6*:(3)56, 1973.
9. Hanson, M.: Motor Performance Testing of Elementary School Age Children. Unpublished Doctoral Dissertation, University of Washington, 1965.

10. Harper, C. J., and Struna, N. L.: Case Studies in the Development of One-Handed Striking. Research Paper, AAHPER meeting, Minneapolis, 1973.
11. Johnson, R.: Measurements of achievement in fundamental skills of elementary school children. Res. Q. Am. Assoc. Health Phys. Educ., *33*:94, 1962.
12. Kitzman, E.: Baseball: electromyographic study of batting swing. Res. Q. Am. Assoc. Health Phys. Educ., *35*:166, 1964.
13. Nieman, R.: A Cinematographical Analysis of Baseball Batting. Unpublished Master's Thesis, University of Wisconsin, 1960.
14. Puck, E.: Mechanical Analysis of Batting in Baseball. Unpublished Master's Thesis, University of Iowa, 1948.
15. Seils, L.: The relationship between measures of physical growth and gross motor performance of primary-grade children. Res. Q. Am. Assoc. Health Phys. Educ., *22*:244, 1951.
16. Sheehan, F.: Baseball Achievement Scales for Elementary and Junior High School Boys. Unpublished Master's Thesis, University of Wisconsin, 1954.
17. Slater-Hammel, A. T.: Action current study of contraction–movement relationships in golf stroke. Res. Q. Am. Assoc. Health Phys. Educ., *19*:164, 1948.
18. Slater-Hammel, A. T.: An action current study of contraction–movement relationships in the tennis stroke. Res. Q. Am. Assoc. Health Phys. Educ., *20*:424, 1949.
19. Wickstrom, R.: Developmental Motor Patterns in Young Children. Unpublished Film Study, 1968.

8

KICKING

Kicking is a unique form of striking in which the foot is used to impart force to a ball. The kick is singled out for special discussion primarily because its highly specialized form makes it the only common form of striking in which the arms do not play a direct role. The types of kicks used most frequently by children in spontaneous play and in organized games are the punt and the place kick. In the punt, the ball is dropped and then kicked before it touches the ground; in the place kick, the ball is stationary when it is kicked. Both types of kicks are included in the following discussion of kicking patterns.

KICKING PERFORMANCE OF CHILDREN

It is somewhat surprising that there have been so few attempts to measure the kicking ability of young children. Gesell reported that a child can kick a ball at age 24 months, and although he mentioned the form that might be used, he did not supply details concerning the procedure for measuring the performance of the 2-year-old.[6] In his discussion of the kicking ability of older children, he described performance in terms of the distance a soccer ball could be kicked through the air. According to Gesell, the 5-year-old can kick the soccer ball a distance of 8 to 11½ feet and the 6-year-old can kick it a distance of 10 to 18 feet. Gesell's report suggests that there is observable kicking behavior at an early age but that kicking performances of children are difficult to measure in quantitative terms before the age of 4 or 5 years. His data also suggest an annual measurable improvement in performance starting approximately at age 5 years.

The 5-, 6-, and 7-year-old children tested by Jenkins recorded successively better mean scores on the soccer kick for distance.[10]

At the respective ages, the mean scores for the girls were 8.0, 10.1, and 15.0 feet and for the boys were 11.5, 18.4, and 25.4 feet. The scores exhibit an increasing superiority for the boys at each of the three age levels. Dohrman also used the soccer kick for distance and found that 8-year-old boys and girls improved significantly in performance between test periods in the fall and spring of the same school year.[5] The boys in Dohrman's study followed the trend of being able to kick farther than girls.

Hanson tested 2840 boys and girls in grades 1 through 6 on the soccer punt for distance, which is a departure from the type of kick used in the previously mentioned studies.[9] Boys' performances exceeded those of girls, and both sexes improved at successive grade levels. Still another type of kicking test was used by Johnson.[11] He measured the kicking accuracy of 624 boys and girls in grades 1 through 6. The children improved in kicking accuracy at each grade level, and the boys were significantly more accurate than the girls at grades 3, 4, and 5. Similarly, Van Slooten's study of performances on motor coordination tasks showed that the boys in the group of 960 six-, seven-, eight-, and nine-year-old children were superior to the girls both in kicking for distance and in kicking for accuracy at each age level.[16] The mean performances of boys and girls improved in each skill at each successive age level.

Although the accumulation of evidence concerning the performances of children in kicking skills is not so massive as it is for other fundamental skills, it nevertheless is diverse and shows a general trend toward annual improvement.

DEVELOPMENTAL FORM IN KICKING

The Place Kick

Gesell indicated that children are ready to kick shortly after they are able to run.[6] His suggestion places the possible starting time at 18 months or at any time after the skill of running has been achieved. In support of this early readiness, Roberts and Metcalf have found that participation of pelvic rotation in the kick over and above that used in running appears to develop as early as at 2 years of age.[14] Despite the early capability, kicking behavior before the age of 2 years is extremely unpredictable and perhaps not worthy of serious classification. If a ball is placed in front of a child and he is encouraged to kick it, his response could vary from running against it or nudging it with his leg, to squatting and hitting it with his hand. The very young child moves against the ball and pushes at it with either leg, making contact at some point on the front part of the lower leg (Fig. 8–1,

FIG. 8-1. Upper: Primal kicking form by a 21-month-old girl. From a short run, she nudges the ball with her left leg and makes a pushing–kicking movement with her right foot. Lower: A 24-month-old boy demonstrates a definite kick with arm opposition and exceptional height on his follow-through.

upper). The movements are haphazard and barely recognizable as a pattern. A child at this age is limited to a pushing action with his leg because lack of balance restricts the leverage of leg movements. Hence, he cannot develop enough force to cause the ball to become airborne unless it is a featherlight beach ball. From this very elementary response, the child begins to show steady progress in kicking behavior (Fig. 8-1, lower).

In her study of the development of motor skill by children, Deach defined kicking as "consisting essentially of a striking movement in which the leg swings through an arc and meets the ball at a more or less advantageous point on the arc."[4] Her observations of the kicking behavior of children ages 2 through 6 years were based upon kicking a stationary ball from a starting position immediately behind it. These conditions for testing kicking behavior encouraged a pendular leg swing and undoubtedly had a significant influence on the four developmental stages Deach identified (Figs. 8-2; 8-3). In the first stage, there was minimal forward movement by the lower leg and little accompanying movement by the arms and trunk. The kicking move-

FIG. 8–2. Upper: Stage I in Deach's sequence. The girl keeps her kicking leg nearly straight and scarcely involves the rest of her body in the movement. Lower: Stage II. Additional leverage for the kick is gained by lifting the lower leg backward and upward in preparation for the kick. There is a small amount of opposition from the arms and slight backward trunk lean. (Drawn from film loaned by Miss Dorothy Deach.)

ment was essentially a forward and upward action with the kicking leg remaining relatively straight at the knee during the entire movement. Characteristic of the second stage was a preparatory backward lift of the kicking foot caused by flexion of the lower leg. The third stage produced a significant increase in the total arc of the leg swing and required a definite compensating movement from the opposite arm. Preliminary extension of the kicking leg at the hip was responsible for the clearly visible increase in leg action. In the final stage of development, greater

FIG. 8-3. Upper: Stage III in Deach's kicking sequence showing increased preliminary extension at the hip, greater arc in the leg swing, and additional body adjustments. Shows slight overcocking of the lower leg. Lower: Stage IV. Effective cocking at the hip and the knee, forceful kicking action requiring backward trunk lean, and extensive arm adjustments during follow-through. (Drawn from film loaned by Miss Dorothy Deach.)

range of motion by the kicking leg occurred in the preparatory as well as in the contributory actions. Additional preparatory hip extension made a more forceful kick possible, which in turn required more extensive compensating movements from the arms and the trunk. Earlier extension of the lower leg coordinated with the movement of the thigh to help effect the more forceful kick.

If the changes in Deach's four stages in kicking were stated in terms of trends, they would include:

1. An increase in the range of preparatory movement at the hip and the knee of the kicking leg.
2. An increase in the total range of motion for the kicking leg.

3. A tendency to start farther behind the ball and move the total body forward into the kick.
4. An increase in compensatory trunk lean and arm opposition.

The overall trend was a gradual change from a relatively straight pendular leg action with little body movement to a sweeping, whiplike leg action with gross body movement.

FIG. 8–4. Upper: A 38-month-old girl demonstrates the typical kick–retract leg motion. She kicks at the ball at this stage rather than through it. Lower: The 34-month-old child runs at the ball, kicks it, and moves forward onto the kicking leg. The kicking-through action is more mature and is encouraged by brisk forward movement prior to the kick.

It is interesting to note that the children in Deach's study almost invariably tended to retract the kicking leg after the completion of the kick. They did not allow leg momentum to carry the rest of the body forward in a follow-through motion. This tendency to withdraw the kicking leg is a clearly identifiable aspect of developmental form in kicking. It can be observed in the early developmental stages of both the place kick and the punt,

though more prominently in the former than the latter. As the child increases the scope and force of his kicking action, he changes from the practice of *kicking at* the ball to the more effective habit of *kicking through* it. The developmental trend of gradually increasing forward body momentum before the kick helps generate a forceful kicking motion and encourages a forward follow-through. The faster the preliminary steps, the greater is the encouragement for the child to kick through the ball. In Figure 8–4, the 38-month-old girl walked toward the ball, kicked it, and then briskly withdrew her kicking foot, thus stopping her forward motion. By contrast, the 34-month-old child in the same illustration ran forward and continued her forward movement after the kick. The difference between the two performances highlights the contribution of quick forward steps to the kick-through technique which is part of the mature pattern. It also is a reminder of the similarity of the movements involved in running and in kicking and the naturalness of combining the two skills. An additional benefit of the forward prekick movement worthy of mention is the potential for more pelvic rotation and a greater distance over which to apply force for the development of velocity of the kicking leg.[3]

During the time the child is developing his kicking skills, he learns that forward movement prior to the kick is the rule rather than the exception. He also learns that kicking through the ball is the way to get greater distance.

In the developmental stages of kicking identified by Deach, the kicking leg is cocked increasingly more, first at the knee and then at the hip.[4] When the child learns he can kick the ball harder and farther by cocking his leg, he frequently exaggerates by overcocking and thereby loses the advantage he intended to gain. Evidence that the lower leg has been overcocked is the closeness of the heel to the back of the thigh as the leg swings forward in the kicking motion. The kicking action of the boy in the lower sequence in Figure 8–3 is an example of this developmental phenomenon. The boy leans forward, hyperextends his thigh, and overcocks his lower leg as his thigh swings forward. At the point where his lower leg should be nearly extended, it is still flexed at almost a right angle. The contribution his thigh makes to the kicking motion is diminished greatly by the delay in the extension of his lower leg. This negative influence of overcocking is overcome gradually as the child realizes that there is a point beyond which further cocking is a hindrance rather than an advantage. He then is ready to regain the full advantage of preliminary cocking at the hip and the knee. As his skill improves, he begins to uncock his lower leg earlier, and his leg becomes increasingly straighter at the knee when the ball is contacted. These important changes in the timing of the kicking movements lead him toward the whipping leg movement of the mature pattern.

As the child continues to develop his kicking skill, he uses a preferred leg more consistently and becomes more adept in adjusting the placement of his support foot as he approaches the ball. Boys seem to begin making successful adjustments in positioning the support foot at an earlier age than girls, according to Deach.[4] The lingering problem of ineffective placement of the support foot is shown in Figure 8–13. Children, ages 5 through 10, are shown at the instant they make contact with the ball. Each has made slightly different adjustments with his body segments because of the position of his support foot relative to the ball, but the common elements of a basic kicking pattern are still evident.

The part of the foot that contacts the ball in the early developmental stages of kicking is determined more by chance than by design. Where the child happens to place his support foot in relation to the ball determines how his foot contacts the ball and how the ball responds to the kick. The child keeps his ankle locked at a right angle during the kick and typically delays the extension of his lower leg, causing his knee to lead the kicking motion. Because there is little variation in these aspects of his kicking pattern, he contacts the ball with his instep if his support foot is close to the ball and with his toes if his support foot is far behind the ball. Both extreme positions of the support foot tend to produce a low trajectory or a rolling ball. The ball should be contacted below its center with the foot swinging in an upward arc to put the ball into flight. If the support foot is planted reasonably close to the ball, it is possible to get an aerial ball by kicking either with the instep or toes, especially when a large, light ball is kicked. The plasticity of this type of ball allows it to compress extensively and stay in contact with the forward-moving foot. By the time it recoils from the foot, upward as well as forward force can be applied to the ball to give it an upward trajectory. An additional advantage of using the light ball is that the child is encouraged to kick forcefully because he need not be afraid of hurting his foot at contact.

The Punt

The punt is a difficult form of kicking for the child because it entails a complex coordination of body movements. He must move his body forward, drop the ball accurately, and then kick it before it touches the ground. The child commonly develops the

movement pattern used in kicking the stationary ball well before he can effectively coordinate the actions of his arms and legs in the punt. In his first attempts at punting, the child characteristically tosses the ball upward in preparation for the kick rather than holding it forward and dropping it (Fig. 8–6). This ineffectual contribution from his arms causes him to contact the ball too far above the ground and he kicks it upward or even

FIG. 8–5. Upper: The 4½-year-old girl drops the ball without taking a preliminary step. Failure to move forward when dropping the ball caused her to contact it near her knee. Lower: She placekicks from a run.

backward over his head. The child's punting performance does not begin to improve rapidly until he learns to drop the ball rather than toss it. Many children respond quickly with more coordinated effort when they are given the suggestion to "hold the ball low and just drop it." Some of the typical coordinations of the actions of the arms and the legs in the punt are illustrated in Figures 8–5, 8–6, and 8–7.

FIG. 8–6. A 4½-year-old boy tosses the ball into the air and waits for it to descend before stepping forward to begin his kicking pattern. The ball eventually drops beyond the toe of his kicking leg despite his reaching effort. His upward toss obscured the possible effectiveness of his kicking pattern.

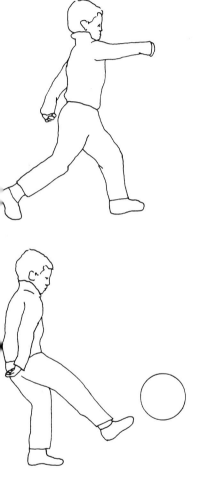

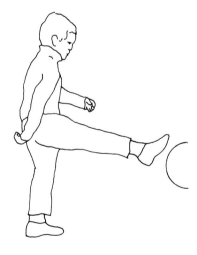

FIG. 8–7. An effective developmental punting pattern. The ball is dropped before the support foot touches the ground and the basic pattern is used. The kicking leg shows exaggerated rotation prior to and incomplete knee extension at contact.

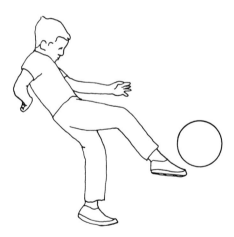

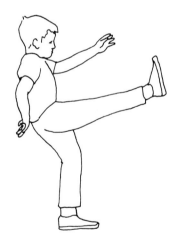

Because of the difficulty of the timing involved in the punt, the skill ordinarily is not expected to be present in an effective pattern until a child is 5 or 6 years old. Yet Halverson and Roberton reported that one of the boys in their longitudinal study unexpectedly demonstrated the ability to punt at age 2 years and 9 months.[8] The child undoubtedly possessed unusual ability, and in addition he probably had an unusually early exposure to the skill. A subsequent study of the punting skill of preschool children furnished further evidence to support the proposal that early development of skill in punting results from early opportunities to observe and to practice it.[17]

Although the available data on the changes in kicking behavior of children are limited, the observations from the longitudinal approach used by Halverson and Roberton and Poe are in general agreement with the observations from the cross-sectional approach used by Wickstrom.[8,13,17] From the findings of these studies, the most prominent developmental changes in the kicking pattern are:

1. More forward movement from steps taken prior to the kick.
2. An increased tendency to drop the ball forward (rather than to toss it upward) in preparation for the kick and to drop it before the support foot is planted.
3. More forceful and extensive action from the kicking leg.
4. More backward trunk lean to accommodate the forward leg movement.
5. Increasingly straighter angles at the knee and ankle at contact.
6. More movement of the kicking leg toward the midline of the trunk in the follow-through.
7. Increasing tendency for the body to continue forward and upward after the kick.

Many of these developmental changes apply to the place kick as well as to the punt and herald positive development toward a mature pattern of kicking.

BASIC PATTERN OF MOVEMENTS IN MATURE KICKING FORM

There seems to be a general pattern consisting of a few movements common to all the basic kicks.[2,7,12,14] "The motions of the leg and thigh in a football punt and place kick follow a pattern very similar to that of a soccer kick. The segments are inclined more forward particularly in the punt since the ball is contacted in the air but the sequence and the rate of motion are very similar in all three kicks."[14]

From the evidence currently available, the movements in the basic mature kicking pattern are:

1. A preliminary forward step on the support leg to rotate the pelvis backward on the opposite side and to extend the thigh of the kicking leg.
2. A forward swing of the kicking leg with simultaneous flexion at the hip and at the knee.
3. Vigorous extension by the lower part of the kicking leg.
4. A momentary cessation of the forward movement of the thigh and continued extension of the lower leg just before the foot contacts the ball.
5. A forward swing of the opposite arm in reaction to the vigorous action of the kicking leg.

This pattern is bone bare and is only suggestive of precise coordination and timing. The pattern gains body by being filled in with the details used in various types of kicks. Precise action of the kicking leg and adjustments by the arms and trunk are determined mostly by two major factors: (1) the intended trajectory of the ball, and (2) the height of the ball from the ground when it is contacted. These factors account for the majority of the special adjustments made by the kicker in the kicking skills used in sports.

USE OF THE BASIC PATTERN OF KICKING IN SPORT SKILLS

The punt and versions of the place kick are prominent skills used in football and in soccer. Skillful kickers in these two sports use a form that is marked by the presence of a common basic pattern with additional movements which are task specific.[14]

The Instep Kick in Soccer

The place kick in soccer is often a goal attempt, and a low trajectory is desired with an emphasis on speed and accuracy. These objectives are achieved by contacting the ball with the instep rather than with the toe. Several important adjustments are made to assure effective instep contact (Fig. 8-8). Starting at an angle which is slightly oblique to the intended direction of the flight of the ball, the kicker takes a short step and then a jump step. Approaching the ball from an angle allows the kicker to shift his weight after the jump step by leaning toward his support leg. With his body leaning in this direction as he kicks the ball, the kicker can swing his leg through a longer arc and still have his instep in correct position for contact.

The kicker places his support foot in an effective position

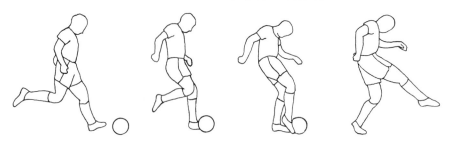

FIG. 8–8. Mature form in the instep kick in soccer. Placement of the support foot and corresponding body adjustments position the instep for contact.

FIG. 8–9. Instep soccer kick by female college soccer player. Compare the features in her movement pattern with those shown in Figure 8–8.

relative to the ball as he lands from the jump step. Placement is to the side of the ball away from the kicking foot and varies from slightly in front of to slightly behind the ball. Adjustments in body movements accommodate small deviations in the placement of the support foot without apparent loss of effectiveness.[2] Before the support foot has touched the ground, the kicking leg begins to flex at the hip and at the knee (Fig. 8–8). At the point in the swing where there is a right angle at the knee and the thigh is past the perpendicular, the lower leg begins its forceful extension. The thigh continues to move forward well ahead of the lower leg, but its forward movement decelerates and finally ceases an instant before the ball is contacted. At contact, the lower leg is approximately perpendicular to the ground and still extending, the ankle is in extension, the trunk is leaning slightly sideward and forward, and the opposite arm is swinging forward in reaction to the movement of the kicking leg. The kicking foot appears to be dragging (Fig. 8–9) because it does not lead the kicking leg as in other place kicks where the toe contacts the ball. The position of the kicking foot at the instant of contact is of vital importance because it dictates the pattern of adjustments characteristic of the instep kick in soccer.

Field Goal Kick in Football

The field goal kick is used to score a point after a touchdown or to score a field goal. There is an urgent need for sharp elevation in the trajectory because of various defensive efforts to interrupt the flight of the ball. The kicker can produce the desired line of flight by contacting the ball well below its center with the toe of his kicking foot when his ankle is locked at a right angle and his foot is moving in an upward arc. Adjustments in many of the movements in his kicking form produce this effective position at the instant of contact.

The two preliminary steps the kicker usually takes help him develop forward momentum, rotate his pelvis, and cock his kicking leg. The first step is the shorter of the two and is followed by a lunge or jump step. At the end of the second step the support foot is placed 6 to 12 inches behind and to the side of the ball so that the kicking leg can swing forward freely (Fig. 8–10). The center of gravity of the body is lowered during the longer step, and then it moves forward and upward during the kicking motion. Before the support foot touches the ground, the thigh of the kicking leg begins to swing forward to develop momentum for the kick. As the thigh swings forward, the hip naturally rotates forward, and the lower leg flexes to reduce the resistance of the forward leg swing and to increase the distance it needs for powerful extension. After the lower leg has been cocked to about a right angle with the thigh, it reverses its action and begins to extend forcefully. The trunk is inclined forward slightly as the thigh is swung forward and upward into position. There is a brief pause in the movement of the thigh immediately before contact, but the lower leg continues to swing forward and upward forcefully. The kicking leg is almost straight at the knee at contact (Fig. 8–10). There is a tendency for the kicking foot to be moving in a slight lateral arc as it comes forward because of the rotation of the pelvis. The leg swings into a groove in the intended direction of the kick before the ball is contacted and

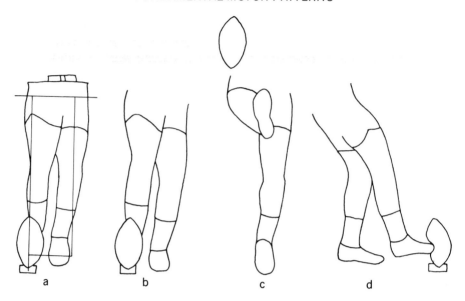

a   b   c   d

FIG. 8–10. Football place kick. Leverage from hip rotation (a), positions of the support and kicking legs at contact, frontal (b) and lateral (d), medialward swing of the kicking leg during follow-through (c). (Redrawn from Becker.[1])

continues in this direction until the ball is airborne. Natural hip rotation moves the kicking leg toward the midline again in the follow-through (Fig. 8–10). Hip rotation contributes significantly to the force developed during the kick, but it must be integrated correctly to avoid a misdirected flight.[1]

The kickoff in football is a minor variation of the place kick pattern. The ball is elevated on a tee prior to the kick, and the objective of the kick is distance rather than a high, arching trajectory. These two special circumstances in the kickoff alter a few of the details in the total pattern of the kick. A longer run in preparation for the kickoff is desirable and is possible because the kicker is not hurried by onrushing defenders. The kicker builds up momentum with his increased run, but the additional forward velocity developed in the process carries him through the kicking position more quickly. He adjusts by placing his support foot farther behind the ball and by decreasing the amount of backward trunk lean prior to the action of the kicking leg. In effect, he kicks more through the ball, and his trunk tends to lean forward during the strong forward follow-through of his kicking leg. The basic but minor differences in the body positions in these two versions of the place kick are apparent in Figure 8–11.

FIG. 8–11. The place kick and the kickoff in football. An extended and vigorous approach in the kickoff develops considerable forward momentum that is transferred to the ball (lower). The emphasis on quick elevation of the ball in the place kick requires less forward lean of the trunk and produces a high rather than forward follow-through (upper).

The Punt

The task of contacting the moving ball above the ground requires adjustments in the kicking pattern that seem to be concentrated in the final phase before contact is made. Nevertheless, the timing and coordination of all the movements must be controlled precisely from the instant the movement pattern begins.

Several of the initial movements in the punt are identical to those used in the place kick. Ordinarily two forward steps precede the kick. The kicker steps forward onto his kicking leg, holding the ball in front of that leg with extended arms. He drops the ball before his support foot touches the ground and his forward motion causes the ball to continue forward in the same direction. The thigh and lower part of his kicking leg begin to flex before his support foot contacts the ground (Fig. 8–12). His support foot lands well in front of his center of gravity, and the

FIG. 8–12. The punt in football. There is a two-step approach, the ball is dropped before the support foot touches the ground, the thigh swings forward, the trunk stays back, and the foreleg is extended at contact.

support leg is nearly straight at the knee. This straight-leg position keeps his trunk well back and not only helps translate his forward motion into angular motion but also allows him to contact the ball well above the ground. Forward rotation of his hip helps to bring his kicking leg forward into position for a powerful kicking action. Forceful extension of the lower leg accompanies decelerating thigh flexion, and the foot is extended at the ankle. At the instant of contact (Fig. 8–12), the thigh stops moving momentarily, the leg is approximately straight at the knee, the trunk is inclined backward, and the opposite arm is forward in reaction to the action of the kicking leg. The center of weight then moves forward and upward, and the kicking leg follows through moving toward the midline of the trunk. If the follow-through is vigorous, the support foot might be lifted off the ground. When this happens, balance is maintained by a short hop on the support foot and by lateral and upward movement of the arms. This total pattern of movements applies equally to the punt in football and to the punt in soccer.

SELECTED MECHANICAL PRINCIPLES IMPORTANT IN KICKING

The following mechanical principles are applicable to the movement pattern of all the common forms of kicking.

1. Linear and angular movements must be integrated for effective performance in many movement patterns (combination of steps and leg swing).
2. Additional linear and angular velocity may be gained by increasing the distance over which force is applied (taking steps and cocking at hip and knee).
3. When several forces are applied in succession, each succeeding force must be applied at the point when the preceding one has made its greatest contribution in imparting velocity (timing of uncocking actions).
4. The potential linear velocity at the end of a lever is increased by increasing the length of the lever (extension of lower leg).

ANALYSIS OF FORM IN KICKING

The basic kicking motion can be acquired relatively early, but the child usually has difficulty using it successfully in childhood games, even when he has control over prekick ball movement. When kicking a stationary ball, he is troubled by effective placement of his support foot; when punting, he has difficulty controlling the drop of the ball. Both problems detract from the effectiveness of the basic kicking pattern. Knowledge of the

FIG. 8–13. Discuss the probable outcome of the flight of the ball for each of the kickers shown at the instant he contacts the ball. What adjustments in body position might produce a more effective kick? Which aspects of the basic pattern of kicking obviously have been used by each?

FIG. 8–14.   The kicking form used by a 4-year-old boy.

problems typically associated with the development of kicking skill can be used to advantage in the analysis of form. Those aspects of the kicking pattern involved in the problems can serve as focal points in the analysis. The observer might try to determine whether the kicker does the following:

Place Kick

1. Takes one or two steps prior to the kick.
2. Places his support foot to the side and slightly behind the ball.

FIG. 8–15. The 9-year-old boy whose kicking form is shown here preferred to kick without shoes.

3. Uses whipping leg action and arm opposition.
4. Follows through with his kicking leg (forward and toward the midline).

Punt

1. Takes one or two preliminary steps.
2. Holds the ball forward and then *drops* it.
3. Uses a whipping leg action and arm opposition.
4. Follows through high and toward the midline with his kicking leg.

FIG. 8–16. A 7-year-old boy punting.

The timing of lower leg extension is a critical feature in mature form, but it occurs in a whipping motion that cannot be dissected by direct observation. Most of the other features are observable and useful in the evaluation of the relative maturity of the kicker's motor pattern. Examination of the sequences in Figures 8–5, 8–6, 8–7, and 8–12 (mature form) for evidence of the features outlined above is good review. Then the kicking sequences in Figures 8–14, 8–15, and 8–16 can be attempted. Finally, analysis must be advanced to the level of using live kickers.

BIBLIOGRAPHY

1. Becker, J.: The Mechanical Analysis of a Football Place Kick. Unpublished Master's Thesis, University of Wisconsin, 1963.
2. Burdan, P.: A Cinematographical Analysis of Three Basic Kicks Used in Soccer. Unpublished Master's Thesis, Pennsylvania State University, 1955.
3. Cooper, J. M., and Glassow, R. B.: Kinesiology. St. Louis, C. V. Mosby Co., 1972.
4. Deach, D.: Genetic Development of Motor Skills in Children Two Through Six Years of Age. Unpublished Doctoral Dissertation, University of Michigan, 1950.
5. Dohrman, P.: Throwing and kicking ability of eight-year-old boys and girls. Res. Q. Am. Assoc. Health Phys. Educ., *35*:464, 1964.

6. Gesell, A.: The First Five Years of Life. New York, Harper & Brothers, 1940.
7. Glassow, R., and Mortimer, E.: Analysis of Kicking. DGWS Speedball-Soccer Guide, 1966–68, AAHPER, Washington, D. C.
8. Halverson, L., and Roberton, M. A.: A Study of Motor Pattern Development in Young Children. Report to the National Convention of the AAHPER, Chicago, 1966.
9. Hanson, M.: Motor Performance Testing of Elementary School Age Children. Unpublished Doctoral Dissertation, University of Washington, 1965.
10. Jenkins, L.: A Comparative Study of Motor Achievements of Children of Five, Six and Seven Years of Age. Teachers College, Columbia University, Contributions to Education No. 414, 1930.
11. Johnson, R.: Measurements of achievement in fundamental skills of elementary school children. Res. Q. Am. Assoc. Health Phys. Educ., *33*:94, 1962.
12. Plagenhoef, S.: Patterns of Human Motion: A Cinematographic Analysis. Englewood Cliffs, N. J., Prentice-Hall, Inc., 1971.
13. Poe, A.: Developmental Changes in the Movement Characteristics of the Punt—A Case Study. Research Abstracts, AAHPER Washington, D. C., 1973.
14. Roberts, E. M., and Metcalfe, A.: Mechanical analysis of kicking. *In* Medicine and Sport, Vol. II: Biomechanics (Wartenweiler, Jokl, and Hebbelinck, eds.). Baltimore, University Park Press, 1968.
15. Smith, W. H.: A Cinematographic Analysis of Football Punting. Unpublished Master's Thesis, University of Illinois, 1949.
16. Van Slooten, P. H.: Performance of Selected Motor Coordination Tasks by Young Boys and Girls in Six Socio-Economic Groups. Unpublished Doctoral Dissertation, University of Indiana, 1973.
17. Wickstrom, R. L.: Developmental Motor Patterns in Young Children. Unpublished study, 1968.

INDEX

207